THE WEARING
OF THE GREEN

Reminiscences of the Glasgow Trams

by William M. Tollan M.A.

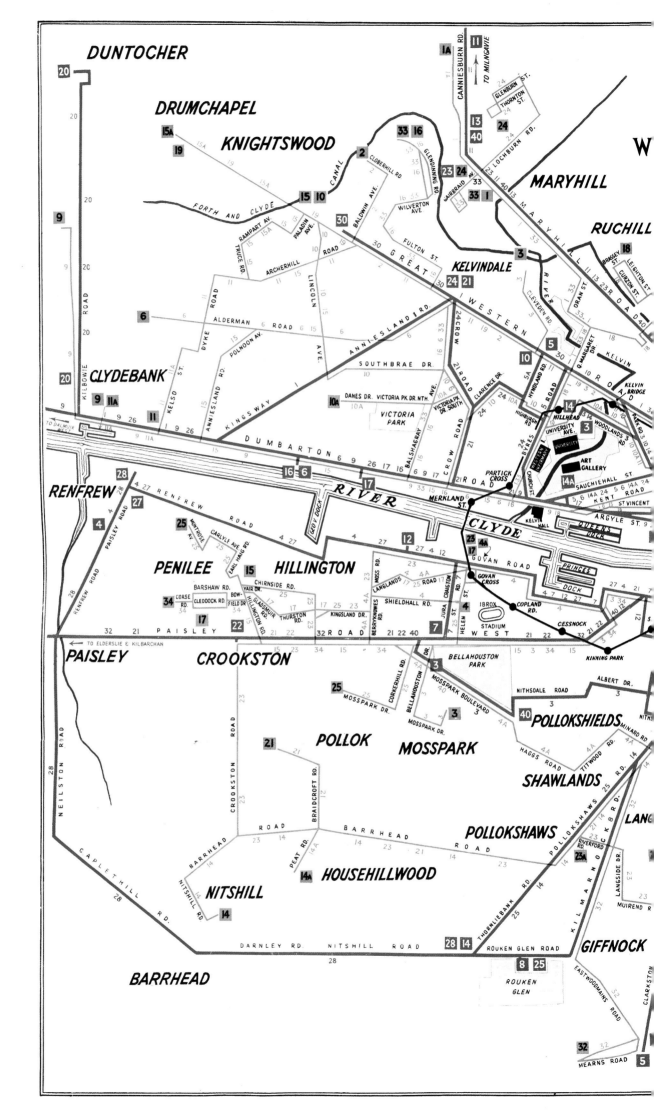

DUNTOCHER

DRUMCHAPEL

KNIGHTSWOOD

MARYHILL

RUCHILL

KELVINDALE

CLYDEBANK

VICTORIA PARK

RENFREW

RIVER CLYDE

PENILEE

HILLINGTON

PAISLEY

CROOKSTON

POLLOK

MOSSPARK

POLLOKSHIELDS

SHAWLANDS

POLLOKSHAWS

NITSHILL

HOUSEHILLWOOD

BARRHEAD

GIFFNOCK

ROUKEN GLEN

2

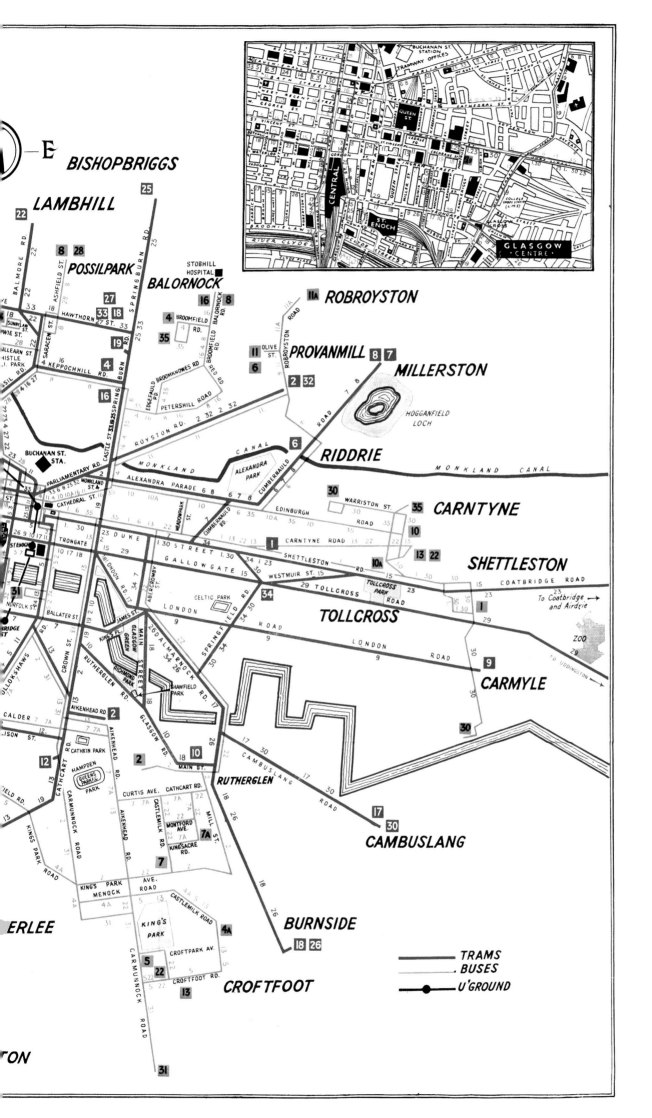

Front cover: short-service motorman, "spare" conductress (has a Bell Punch instead of the more usual Ultimate Ticket Machine) and long service point cleaner at Auchenshuggle Terminus posing with Coronation Mark One car 1151 which was built in 1938 and scrapped in 1962.

A catalogue entry for this book is available from the British Library.

ISBN 1 874422 27 3

Publication no. 29

Published 2000 by
Adam Gordon,
Priory Cottage,
Chetwode,
Nr. Buckingham,
MK184LB

Printed by Drogher Press, Unit 4, Airfield Way, Christchurch, Dorset BH23 3TB

Typesetting and design by Trevor Preece, Gawcott, Buckingham.

CONTENTS

THE WEARING OF THE GREEN

The motorman's operating position on a Glasgow Standard car. This is the more favoured Metropolitan Vickers controller with air-brake interlock box fitted. The controller direction handle is in the forward position, with both motors in circuit. The dual purpose air gauge can be seen bottom right.

Coronation Mark 2 car (more commonly known as a "Cunarder") passing Celtic Park – and not a motor-car in sight. This is the second Celtic ground pre-Lisbon Lions and pre Fergus McCann. It received the nick-name "Paradise" because the first ground on the other side of Janefield Street had been adjacent to a cemetery. The floodlight pylons were supposed to be the tallest in Europe and it was not unknown at matches for the odd (very!) show-off to climb a pylon and perform handstands and other acrobatic feats on the very top itself. Rather him than me. *(see page 24)*

Parkhead's 435 on service 30 in that dismal part of Cambridge Street where I would alight for St. Aloysius' College, wondering if my homework would pass muster. *(see page 24)*

Tool van W27, ex-Paisley 1005, at Coplawhill Works. This was open-fronted until 1938 and one of these coming up Westmuir Street led to my boyhood ambition to be the proud motorman in charge of a works' car. *(see page 11)*

Standard at Sauchiehall Street/Renfield Street. Before the war, the Lambhill service used Renfield Street, going straight on up to Cowcaddens, whereas all other services using Renfield Street would turn left or right. So a young points-boy was employed at the junction to change the three points accordingly. I always thought it a pretty dangerous situation for the boy. Someone at head Office must have been of the same opinion, for the Lambhill cars were altered to go up to Cowcaddens via Hope Street and an Electric Point was put in for right or left turns.
On one occasion the Traffic Lights controlling the Crossing failed on "Red", and the motorman at the head of the long line of cars delayed on Renfield Street, who happened also to be a Special Constable, used his initiative and went on through the red light in order to get the trams moving again. For his pains the motorman was booked by the police and fined in court.
Sure enough, some months later, the same motorman found himself in the same situation. This time the Police pleaded with him to move on through the lights. You can imagine the response they received.
There was sometimes a Head Office messenger stationed hereabouts to receive and distribute paperwork to and from depots.

Dedicated to Motorman John Tollan and all the GCT platform staff who served Glasgow and its surrounding area so well and ably, and remembering with affection that they took such great care of the children they transported to schools, parks and countryside.

John Tollan posing in front of the Children's Museum in Tollcross Park.

For material assistance and aid in preparing this book I am most grateful to Gerard Eadie and his assistant Mrs Avril McCaffrey of C.R. Smith, Dunfermline; Ronnie Fulton, partner in HBM Sayers, and William Kane of Uddingston. I also must acknowledge Gordon Findlay of Uddingston, who with much patience and good humour corrected my computer mistakes. I also thank Willie Guthrie of East Kilbride, Ian Coonie of Paisley, Father David Tudor of St. George's-in-the-Meadows, Nottingham and many National Tramway Museum members for their welcome advice, suggestions and encouragement; and, of course, that most kind motorman Hamilton Brown...

GREEN FOR PARKHEAD
MEMORIES ARE MADE OF THIS

There was a pleasant accompaniment to life as I first experienced it. Just under the windows of our front room the bow collectors of Glasgow trams would hiss soothingly on the overhead wire accompanied by a gentle "thump-thump" as their wheels crossed the track-joints. It was comforting last thing at night and first thing of a morning for this child to hear the message and to know that all was still well with the world.

But on occasion there would be a low rumbling and grinding noise and I would run to the Shettleston-facing window to see a large green tram-car right up on the pavement outside the building. I would watch in fascination as disgruntled men in green uniforms would struggle to put the errant monster back on its lines. Not that I knew it then, but that must have been during the unsuccessful attempts by GCT to operate the 1090-1140 series of double-bogie cars on the Airdrie-Paisley service. We lived in Westmuir Street, Parkhead, right at its junction with Shettleston Road. It was this very junction that gave Shettleston its mediaeval origin as Scheddenstoun. And the junction was still sometimes referred to by locals as the sheddens. Watching the passing "caurs" – as I grew older I was genuinely surprised to find they were actually "tram-cars" – was a fascinating pastime for a child. Going to town the motormen would usually be ahead of time and would coast down Westmuir Street or Shettleston Road, often studying their time-boards as they went, for there was little other road traffic about in those days. Coming out of town the trams would be pelting at great speed to the junction, particularly those flying up Shettleston Road. The motormen of these cars had had a lengthy run up from the Rigby Street stop and they would be on top parallel right to the junction. They would then smartly throw-off and brake perfectly over the Carntyne cross-over for the Muiryfauld Drive stop. I was always amazed they didn't derail. But what driving skill and judgement. No 4mph on crossings with these speedsters. No wonder the standard truck frames kept fracturing with such abuse. Of course I didn't know then it was dreadful driving practice and just thought it all wonderful and longed for the day when I could emulate my

Shettleston Road at Westmuir Street junction. Looking down what we knew as the "back" road where the 23 service went straight on into the city via Dennistoun and the 15 went left to the city via Parkhead. As a youth, Tommy Docherty lived in the tenement on the right. The great Beardmore's works occupies the background.

Coronations in Shettleston Road looking towards Westmuir Street junction and the Carntyne cross-over for Beardmore's specials. I was brought up in Westmuir Street behind Di Duca's garage on the right. There was usually a great display of large cars to be examined. The large building on the left was part of the huge Beardmore's steelworks and was known to us as "the howitzer shop". The "face" in the middle distance was the local lamp-lighter's office. The surrounding tenements had gas lighting.

James St. Bridge, one of GCT's 17 river crossings. This is where Hammy wanted to have his sit-down. That week-day things were much busier than on this peaceful Sunday view. Standard 318 was built in 1909 and scrapped in 1958 and spent all of its 50 years attached to Dennistoun Depot. (see page 42)

10

heroes. The Carntyne cross-over was there for specials arranged for the workers in Beardmore's vast steel-works. As I grew a little older I became aware of differences in the trams. Some had one magnetic shoe dangling between the wheels, others had two. Some had round fronts, others had angled panels. Some had different types of axle-box covers, and sometimes these were mixed on the same car. The big treat was to see the appearance of a sombre red-painted works car, and the glory of glories was when one of Glasgow's wonderful illuminated cars would appear. If one of these went up towards Shettleston I could not be prised away from the window until it had re-appeared heading to the city again. This was the ultimate ambition. To drive an illuminated car. How did one come to gain such exalted status? A great man indeed to be taking such glory round the city. Being on the famous Airdrie-Paisley line, there

Works Cars 3, 20 & Cable Car at Coplawhill Works. So did you know that Glasgow operated a Cable Car? No. 1 was purposely built for the cable operation but was not pulled by a cable as in San Francisco but pulled cables instead – into and out of cable ducts. What remains of it is at the National Tramway Museum Store at Clay Cross, Derbyshire. 3 was a mains testing car converted for that purpose from "Room & Kitchen" car 672. It has now been restored to quasi-original condition and may be seen in the Glasgow Transport Museum as representative of Glasgow's first purpose-built fleet of American style electric cars. No.20 was a Mains department Tool Van converted from Paisley car 39.

were many different names to be spotted on the destination screens. Where was Bargeddie or Whitevale, or what was Halfway between?

Gradually a picture of the service complications began to emerge. City-wards, a Queen Street would be followed by an Ibrox, then would come a Crookston and a Paisley West. Outbound a Shettleston would precede a Baillieston which would be followed by an Airdrie. That was on our "front road". On the "back road" as we called the Airdrie-Knightswood service, St. Vincent Place might be followed by Kelvinside then Anniesland before Knightswood appeared. In the evening rush hour many additional names appeared on the car blinds.

NEWLANDS FAR AWAY

Eventually I had to attend St. Mark's Primary School in Muiryfauld Drive. This large red-sandstone building could be seen from the house, so there was no excuse for being late. In fact it was just possible to wait in the house for the school-bell to ring its clarion call and then make a breenge down stairs and over back-courts and get in the class line before the teacher appeared. One day the teacher (Miss Macnabola – who could forget that name- but she was very nice!) announced that as a special treat for the King's Coronation, we were going to the park for the day. I remember feeling decidedly miffed by that announcement. For by that time I spent much time in the adjoining park – Tollcross Park – and couldn't quite see what the excitement was all about. Then came the great day, and much to my amazement the whole school made a crocodile waddle down to the fare stage in Shettleston Road. There I found it hard to believe what I was seeing. Could it really be four red cars? Never before or since were four red cars to be seen together on Shettleston Road. Wasting no time on

manners and good order and discipline I was upstairs on the front car like a shot and ensconced on the Glaswegian's favourite place – right on the front seat out on the box above the motorman's platform. As we ran quickly up to Parkhead Cross and headed down the Gallowgate, I became fascinated by the gentle hisses coming from the air-brake, for as I was later to learn, these red cars were semi-modernised cars kept in Newlands Depot for special workings and they retained the Saxby straight-air brake. I suppose the lovely sighs of that air-brake on that journey was the moment I became completely hooked on trams for life. Going along Argyle Street I had another astonishment. Lo! and Behold! We turned left at Glassford Street. Although these curves were used by Dennistoun, Parkhead and Coatbridge cars going to and from Coplawhill Works I was never again to see them used in passenger duty. At Gorbals Cross all four motormen met and had a summit conference by the front platform of the leading car. I've often wondered what that heated discussion could have been about. Our destination was Rouken Glen and the route should have been straight-forward enough. Maybe that the first motorman was not going through the notches fast enough for the other three motormen? The next excitement was to come into a road with trees along it. Then a tram-depot appeared surrounded with trees. What sort of world was this? I thought till then that trees only grew in Tollcross Park or out in the country. But round a tram depot? Of course this was Newlands depot we were passing. Of Rouken Glen and the rest of the day I have no memory at all. But the joy of that trip on the old Saxby has never left me. May be heaven will be an eternal ride on a Saxby car passing depots with trees. And Coronations.

A "magnetic" point was installed at the Shettleston Road/Westmuir Street junction. The "clonk" as it went over at the motorman's whim (well usually!) was fascinating. (Question: Where and when was the first ever magnetic point installed?).

THE ELEVENTH HOUR
In the thirties a moving tribute was still being observed. Beardmore's various sirens would bellow and the passing trams would respectfully come to a halt with the crews standing beside their vehicles, uniformed hat held across the chest. For it was eleven o'clock on the eleventh of November and everyone alive then had relatives and friends who had been killed in the war to end wars. No doubt the green staff knew employees lost in Dalrymple's ill-fated battalion. After two minutes the sirens blared again, the crews took up their appointed places and traffic began moving. I always found it to be a moving experience. A pity the custom was not restarted after 1945.

OUCH!
But an unpleasant childhood memory remains. Carried upstairs on a blue car in Paisley Road, I had my head well and truly rattled on the brown wooden weather shield. So now the secret is out as to how my brains became so addled.

GIVE US SOME AIR
A later memory of being with my father on trams is of boarding a tram going down Westmuir Street from Parkhead Cross. He then joined several tramwaymen who were sitting on the front stairs and there were others gathered on the platform with the motorman. All very unusual for Glasgow. They were interested in the mysteries of the new inter-locked controller/air-brake system being operated. And all this on a service car. A bonus was to follow. On a Sunday afternoon we walked over to Parkhead Depot. Here a lye had been cleared of all cars except for one fitted-out with the new inter-lock system. Father had plenty of time to try his hand up-and-down the lye and after he was satisfied with his own ability, I was allowed half-a-dozen shots. And so came about the first time I drove a tram-car. But not the last. What a Sunday that was. I could only have been six or seven at the time.

PARKHEAD DEPOT
Although one of Glasgow's smaller depots, Parkhead was one of the most interesting. In the thirties its cars, as well as serving the city itself, also took their crews to other outlying towns and villages. Airdrie, Coatbridge, Baillieston, Paisley, Clydebank, Uddingston and later Rutherglen and Cambuslang (once claimed to be the largest village in Scotland) were normal destinations, so life was quite varied for the platform staff. Airdrie to Paisley West covered over twenty miles of very varied territory as well as being partly an inter-urban service. A double Airdrie-Paisley run was a day's duty. At one time only two minutes were allowed at the termini, so eating and drinking had to be done "on the move". There were numerous varieties of short-workings but the one dad really hated was a week involved in only Shettleston to Queen Street trips (Queen Street lye was in Argyle Street opposite where Lewis emporium was built). I knew he would be very grumpy that week and made a special effort to be on best behaviour. There was one day off per week, Sunday alternating with Monday to Friday. It was not till Sir Patrick Dollan's reforms of working conditions that Saturday was included, but even then only every twelve weeks. Parkhead was the replacement depot for Whitevale, and the latter's War Memorial had been brought up to Tollcross Road and re-erected at the depot entrance. Parkhead had also been given GCT's recreation facilities and as well as a large billiard hall, the adjoining Sports Grounds extended to Helenvale Street, almost at Parkhead Cross. The turf of the football pitch was regarded as among the best in Scotland and Celtic FC trained there for a time in the fifties and sixties, so good old GCT played no small part in the glory that was Lisbon. When King George VI was still Duke of York, he celebrated the opening of the depot and its facilities by laying a wreath at the War Memorial and he then drove 38 from the depot to

The great Dalrymple is the one with the Imperial beard. The General Manager looks worried about his car in the hands of York. But where was the white rose?

Parkhead's 14 at Tollcross. This detested car is on its way to Broomhouse. Hope it managed to stop there. The traction poles are still extant fifty years on. Glasgow's last horse tram line worked from Tollcross to Parkhead. Note section insulators in the overhead. Power had to be "off" passing the insulators especially during the wartime blackout as otherwise massive arcing would take place with consequent damage to the insulators.

Parkhead Cross. So 38 was thereafter known as 'the royal car'. The Royal signature "Bertie" is still to be seen in the Depot Visitor's Book.

The Transport Sports Day held annually at Parkhead was in the top rank in its time, with world Champions performing for us. In view of modern developments, I wish I had misspent my youth on the fine billiard tables, but I only had the occasional game on their excellent surfaces and was no match for the old man's skills.

A HOO-DOO CAR?

If 38 was "the royal car", 14 was the most detested car. No motorman wanted to drive it, for no matter what attention was given to it, its brakes were not reliable. Of course I thought that just an old wives' tale. And yet , and yet... There I was in the 'fifties sitting out on its front box going down the Gallowgate and we were missing every stop by miles. The language coming up the front stairs was unprintable.

BUDDIES, KILLIES AND PSEUDO-DUNEDINS

Much better regarded and thought to be the speediest of the cars – and the much the easiest to operate – were two ex-Paisley low-height cars 1056 and 1057. Strangely there were also two of the double-bogie cars, 1100 and I think 1106. I remember asking paterfamilias why Parkhead had them in view of their disastrous penchant for derailment (I had often heard his stories of alarmingly crabbing side-

ways down Glasgow Road hill while attempting to use the Barrachnie cross-over). Apparently Parkhead had high-loading specials that required their use and certainly when I was going off to take school football on a Saturday morning, one of them would be heading east to Bargeddie. I don't think they were allowed beyond there. To my lasting regret I always intended to make the run with it but never quite got round to actually doing it.

Even within the Standards there were variations. Apart from a choice of round-dash / hex-dash fronts, controllers could vary between the preferred Metrovic brand, English Electric or GEC. Some had an extra weak-field notch gained by pushing down on the controller handle when the final top parallel notch had been attained. A few cars had experimentally been fitted with pantographs instead of the ubiquitous Fischer bow-collectors. Number 2 was one of these. At one time several cars had livery variations. Edinburgh-style streamlining appeared and there were cars painted with a narrow colour-band above the large green.

I wasn't allowed down into the maintenance pits which ran the lengths of the lyes – much as I would have liked to do that – I never managed to get under a Standard until John Shawcross & Co. gave me that privilege at the National Tramway Museum at Crich in Derbyshire, but I did have the fun of climbing up on to the top-deck washing gantries to read at close quarters the via boards positioned on the sides of the Standards in the mid-thirties. At the back of the depot were the sand bins but not much in the way of engineering equipment. There was a large hand-

13

Sett Wagon W37 at Coplawhill, built new in 1937 using truck from 791. *(see page 11)*

Standard at Kelvinbridge, with the great Episcopal Cathedral of George Gilbert Scott and John Oldrid Scott quite outdone in height by the 208 foot spire of John Honeyman's Lansdowne Church. Here trams passed over the River Kelvin, the Underground, a suburban railway and street. So the Underground was unusual for Glasgow in having two entrances at two different levels. The railway from Central Station was used to bring guests from the Caledonian Railway's Central Station Hotel to Caledonian Mansions (on the far left side of the Bridge) which was used as an annex to that Hotel. *(see page 53)*

Coronation Mark One leaving Parkhead Depot with the post-war track alterations to accommodate the car-wash. Two "All cars stop here" signs were erected at the depot gates to remind crews that the conductor or conductress was to precede the car on to Tollcross Road. Had no-one at Head Office ever heard of traffic lights? I suppose it was cheaper to get a new employee. There is a puzzle about this picture as the tram is on the wrong track for exiting to "Maryhill" as shown on the destination screen.

worked grindstone on which dad would occasionally sharpen our kitchen knives. In the innocence of childhood I thought that a bit unfair on the itinerant knives-sharpener who used to do a regular round in Parkhead streets. Entry into Parkhead Depot for trams was economically made from Tollcross Road by means of two single-line trailing junctions. (Years later I was highly amused to see the entry into STEFER's Rome Depot on the Appian Way. In the latter case the running lines were quadrupled past the "deposito" and entry was by two double track junctions. Initial costs and maintenance must have been very high for the Belgian Company. Of course they may have had shares in a steel mill!)

Inside Parkhead's yard forecourt the single line entrances formed double track and each track led to its own set of sidings. But, craftily, in the middle of the double-track was a scissors crossing so that any car entering could arrive at any of the Depot lyes. In addition the scissors crossing could be by-passed by means of a loop line alongside the boundary wall. At the end of the loop line was a short siding. Sometimes a works car or a disabled car or even an accident-damaged car might be on the siding or loop awaiting a journey to Coplawhill. The entry/exit lay-out of course meant that all cars had to reverse in Tollcross Road to come into the Depot, but cars going out on service towards the Uddingston, Paisley and Cambuslang direction had a straight run at it. However, for cars heading out of the Depot for duties in the Shettleston or Duke Street direc-

tions, the lay-out at Parkhead Cross meant that these cars had to reverse on one of the cross-overs beyond the Cross to head back in the correct direction. To reach either cross-over, Parkhead Depot cars had to run over three junctions at Parkhead Cross at Westmuir Street, Duke Street and Springfield Road. Usually they turned on the one at the top of Springfield Road, rarely on the Gallowgate one. Then of course the cars had to come back over the junctions. Conversely trams returning home from Shettleston or Duke Street had to reverse the process. So Parkhead Cross could be pretty busy and became additionally so after the war when a double-track connection was installed from Gallowgate into Springfield Road. A high points box was erected on the corner of Westmuir Street and Tollcross Road to help reduce tram congestion and ease motormen's problems. No wonder GCT was reluctant to have Lanarkshire system cars coming into the city via Parkhead. Eventually a crew bothie was established in the Gallowgate just opposite to where St. Michael's Church now stands. Last time I looked it had become a Doctor's surgery.

WASH THE CHANGES!

After the war the double-track with scissors-crossing in the Parkhead Depot fore-court was replaced by a single line complete with a drive-through car-wash appliance. I often wondered what a motorman felt like taking an open-platform Standard through a wash. Dad had taken his last ride to the big depot in the sky by that time so I never found out.

A Standard and a Coronation Mark One at Parkhead Cross. *(see page 15)*

HERE COME DE TRAM!

Another extraordinary thing happened. Two of our familiar red passenger "All cars stop here" tablets appeared on the two last traction poles inside the depot gates and the instruction was issued that all trams leaving the Depot had to be pulled up at these signs. The conductor or conductress had then to alight and lead the tram out of the Depot on to Tollcross Road. That would be a real treat in wet weather. Did Bath Street issue red flags as well? Had no one in Head Office heard of traffic lights? I suppose it was cheaper to have an injured person than spend a bit of money on safety. And what did the single motorman on a works car do?

NICE CARNATION!

In those far-off days, for years the Parkhead Head Depot Clerk was a rather imposing chap known respectfully to my dad as Mr Scaife. He was always to be seen with a carnation on his lapel. One morning I was delighted to find him sitting on a Standard I was conducting coming up Springfield Road. Knowing full well who he was and where he was going, I loudly repeated "Fares Please!" in his lughole. He pompously expressed the opinion that he did not pay fares. Inwardly chuckling, I responded that he would have to pay a fare, alight, or have an uncollected fare form issued. He then grudgingly produced a gold pass and I, of course, could not resist asking him how he obtained such a thing. I was recently walking Jimmy the Woof past Parkhead Depot, and I went in to have a sentimental look.

It was now a bus garage and in recent years I asked the courteous gateman if I could visit the War Memorial. I was staggered to find that the First War memorial to the tramwaymen who had died for us was no longer there and the gateman had never heard of it. (However, Charles McDonald, the Parkhead historian, and Brian Longworth of the Summerlee Transport Group, tell me that in fact the War Memorial, [along with other GCT War Memorials] is in a Garden of Remembrance behind the Depot. This good gesture to our dead was arranged at the suggestion of the transport union.) The friendly gateman also told me that the site was being sold and houses were to be built on the site. So what had been built and paid-for by the Glasgow ratepayers and served the West of Scotland so faithfully was now going to put more money into the pockets of the financiers. Such is progress in our dismal times. But at least they cannot take my happy memories of Parkhead Depot.

WE STILL HAD AN EMPIRE

Among the many thrills of the thirties, the biggest was the still much-talked-about Empire Exhibition of 1938 dominated by the illuminated Tait's tower. That the tower was lost after the Exhibition closed is still a source of great disappointment to those who knew it. With that great Exhibition came the most comfortable public service vehicle ever built – the justly famous Coronation tramcar. We sometimes travelled into town to savour the early pair on the Mosspark/University service when they first came into

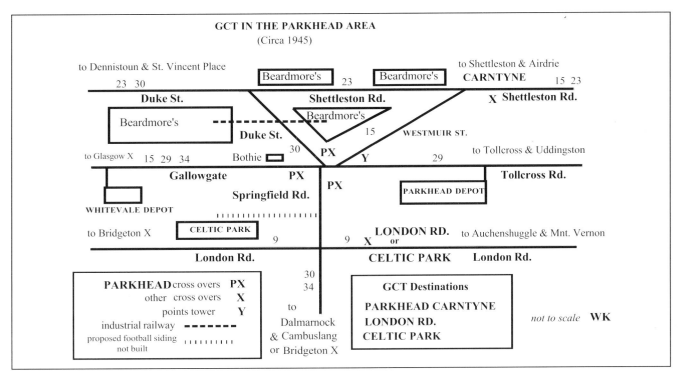

GCT IN THE PARKHEAD AREA
(Circa 1945)

service. 1142 was quite extraordinary in appearance and really look to me somewhat ungainly when compared to what the class finally looked like. I was truly open-mouthed when I first saw it in its first fussy red, blue and silver grey livery. The Maley and Taunton style bogies didn't help its looks (and I always felt they spoiled the looks of the ex-Liverpool cars too.). But what a ride 1142 gave. I was jealous of the fact that it wasn't on the premier Airdrie-Paisley service. 1141 was more like the thing appearance-wise. Truly a classic piece of engineering and styling. Well! For the passengers. The front end and driver's cab left a bit to be desired. The cab was draughty and cramped. Even today you can still tell a genuine GCT motorman – for he sits sideways at the controls. (This was so that a motorman could vacate the cramped cab more quickly in an emergency situation.)

WHAT THE MOTORMAN SAID

Eventually Parkhead had its share of the class, and indeed more than its share when the wartime Luftwaffe threat caused the valuable Coronations to be evacuated from the riverside depots of Partick and Lorne School, Govan. I suppose someone in authority had forgotten that Parkhead was adjacent to the giant Beardmore's plant and the great Clydebridge Steelworks. My father said that originally the first cars had been fitted with a microphone and loud-speaker system so that the motorman could advise passengers of the stops, but that this had had to be removed after several occasions when horse-carters had delayed the tram by doing the usual Glasgow carter thing of using the tram rails to ease the burden on their Clydesdales, and were accordingly addressed by the motormen in decidedly unparliamentary language – with the system switched on. Dad also knew that the new big cars were causing problems because they were over-taxing the power supply – particularly on the country sections.

AT THE FRONT END

Attending the Empire Exhibition brought the excitement of watching special cars of all sorts and colours working the special circular routes (30/30a) to Bellahouston from St. Vincent Street going out along Paisley Road and returning round the Park via Dumbreck to the city and vice versa.

After one visit to the Exhibition, I wondered where we were walking to. It turned out to be Cessnock Underground Station. When the train came in, my father knew the driver who was kind enough to take me into the cab and to "let" me drive the train round to St. Enoch's. Mind you I'm sure he did it all really! But I thought this was the life for me. At every station the Station-Master would put his head into the cab and stare at me. And each time came the same joke. "Not him again, is it?" So it must have been a fairly normal treat given by the Underground staff to wee Glaswegians in 1938. Couldn't happen today, could it?

G-GOING W-WITH A S-S-PLASH

During the school holidays, I was often shunted off to do the Airdrie-Paisley run with my father, and his very pleasant conductor, James Kelly. Jimmy had a stutter and a great liking for Irish Sweepstake tickets. James would eat with us sometimes because of the often short duty breaks, and I well remember him laying a Sweepstake ticket down on our kitchen table and pronouncing: "W-w-w-william! I-I-If th-th-th-this t-t-t-ticket wins, y-your f-f-f-father is s-s-s-stopping the c-c-car on J-J-Jamaica B-b-b-bridge and the b-b-bag is g-g-g-going in-in-in-into the C-C-C-Clyde, th-th-th-th-th-the p-p-p-p-punch is g-g-g-going into- th-th-the C-C-C-Clyde, and the u-u-u-u-niform is g-g-g-going into the C-C-C-Clyde". That would have been one for Dennis Gill's "On the Trams!" (Which reminds me that a conductor, when asked if his car went over Jamaica Bridge, is said to have responded that he hoped not – as he was averse to getting wet. Sorry!)

Parkhead's 69 showing Uddingston as a destination.

IT'S A LONG WAY TO GO

But the twenty miles of Airdrie-Paisley only cost one old penny, for in the summer months children could ride any distance on the cars for one old penny. Of course the fare was always properly paid by me – but I always got to punch the ticket. Once, when a bit older, I travelled to Paisley Cross, caught a blue tram and came back to the city through Barrhead. Then I caught a green tram again for home. All for three old pennies. And for the same price of three old pennies I had a more extended day, going in the opposite direction but extending the blue car run this time to Renfrew Ferry. Crossing on the Ferry to Yoker I caught a "back-road" green car back to Parkhead Cross. Who needed computers and TV?

WHAT ODA STARTED

My favourite run of all though, was out along Hamilton Road and through the fields and woods to Uddingston with its justly famed Tunnock's Bakery and Tea-rooms. . It was a great change to leave dirty, noisy, industrial, tenement and public-house ridden Parkhead, and go out through the countryside, with its mansions, woods, fields and river, to the delightful little village – as Uddingston then was. Uddingston is said to mean 'the homestead of Uda (or Oda)', which is a bit puzzling, since Oda (or Uda!) is an Angle name. Uddingston once had its own Saint – St. Molaise, whose church site was extant as recently as the building of the Caledonian Railway main-line embankment from the Clyde Bridge in 1852, which duly covered it. Certainly there was a Bronze Age settlement at Kylepark by the Clyde, and a Roman road passed by on the east side of the present M74 motorway. Not many saints but a lot of sinners around these days. Uddingston was once world-famous for producing well-made ploughs. Today, perhaps, apart from producing masses of marshmallows, among other things, it is a noted Call Service and Cable TV centre.

WHERE CROMWELL CAME CALLING

Sometimes the tram ride was followed by a long (for my wee legs!) walk to picturesque Bothwell Castle, open to visitors at that time only on Wednesday afternoons, although there were set-aside picnic areas in the grounds. Today the 13th Century Walter de Moravia (Walter Murray), Red Douglas and Black Douglas stronghold is open daily and still as rewarding of a visit as ever. The beautiful policies were owned by the Douglas-Home family till the twenties. At GCT's Uddingston terminus, White, Blue, Red or Yellow cars – as opposed to the usual Green – might be lying over on the long track over-laps beyond the cross-over, as excursion trips to Bothwell Castle would come from all over the GCT system. To this day, long-term residents still speak of Uddingston as "The Village" (although that status has long gone what with numerous housing and industrial estate developments in the surrounding area) and its cricket team has always been nick-named "The Villagers". Up to the Hitler war years Uddingston was so small in size that mail was addressed not to streets in Uddingston but merely to named buildings. In the halcyon days of my youth, Uddingston's service cars could come from as far as Paisley West – quite a lengthy journey.

Later Airdrie and Uddingston services were started from Ferguslie Mills and then from even further West, from Elderslie itself. In the latter case cars started from a cross-over short of the Depot terminus. In my father's early GCT days the service only ran over the Paisley system from a lye on the West side of Paisley Cross itself. This lye was sited on the Renfrew side of the street and involved a little complicated track-work. The Paisley West lye (which replaced the Paisley Cross one) lay between the running lines and I once saw the singular bogie pattern car 142 resting in the lye as we passed by. As well as Parkhead, (a depot which replaced the old Whitevale Depot on the task), Elderslie and Lorne School Depots contributed their quotas of cars to the route. Shorter workings in rush hours might come from Ferguslie Mills, Paisley West, Paisley Cross, Crookston, Halfway (later replaced by Corkerhill Road), Ibrox, Paisley Road Toll, Queen Street, Glasgow Cross or Parkhead itself. Crookston and Ibrox were the most used for short workings. When I first became aware of such a thing, the service number displayed (on boards then!) was 15a – as the service was regarded as an adjunct to the celebrated Airdrie-Paisley service 15. At one period Uddingston cars had operated to Maryhill (a fore-runner of things to come?) by way of the Gallowgate and Argyll Street to the Glassford Street half-Grand Junction where they turned up Glassford Street to George Square and thence via West Nile Street to Cowcaddens. I certainly don't remember that period, but this was what paterfamilias said he had done on the service, and I have since seen the occasional picture of trams doing that variation of GCT's Uddingston service. (I have looked long and hard to find a picture of a maximum traction double-bogie car in Uddingston – but without success. They must have reached the Village as they were intended for the Uddingston run? Does anyone have such a record?).

WHAT WE LOST

But why did GCT choose to reach out to such a tiny outpost as Uddingston? There would be the customary generous GCT response to a community request, but no doubt the tramway grapevine would also have made known the intention of the Lanarkshire Tramway Company to lay rails from Hamilton via Bothwell to Uddingston. A time-tabled through service was consequently to be advertised from Glasgow city centre to various Lanarkshire tramways including Hamilton and Motherwell.

COME AWAY THE...

Such a service was especially welcomed by football fans from Glasgow clubs going to Motherwell's Fir Park and Hamilton Accies' Douglas Park football grounds, and vice versa, while Hamilton Racecourse Meetings also provided much traffic. Service 15 took fans – for a few coppers – to Broomfield Park, Airdrie; Albion Rovers' Coatbridge Ground at Cliftonhill; Parkhead's famous Celtic Park as well as Ibrox; and St. Mirren's, Love Street stadium in Paisley; and Junior football grounds too numerous to mention. 15a from Uddingston served Parkhead, Ibrox and Love Street, and also Paisley Ice Rink. Villagers were quite accustomed to the run to Paisley and back for a night on the ice. No wonder there were massive football attendances at Senior and Junior matches in the West of Scotland in pre-

Last day of service in Uddingston. The tenement building behind the right-hand traction pole is known to this day in Uddingston as "the electric building" as it was the first in the Village to be supplied with electricity. (W. Guthrie).

My favourite car at my favourite terminus (W. Guthrie).

Television days with such cheap, reliable and frequent public transport.

CORONATIONS ALL THE WAY

GCT reached Uddingston's Caledonian Station (three Uddingston railway stations then, with yet another three adjacent!) in May 1907, with the final terminus at the Cross being reached a month later. When coming home on RAF leave, courtesy of an LMS Coronation, it was amazing how often one of our marvellous Coronations would be on the overbridge at Uddingston Station as the express slowed for the Clyde Bridge slack. A most welcoming sight that was. On reflection, the sight of a Coronation on war-time service to Uddingston should have been expected, as Partick and Lorne School [Govan] Depots were adjacent to the docks and these two Depots had been denuded of the expensive and modern Coronations in case of bombing attacks on docks and shipyards, so that Parkhead would have had loads of Coronations available for the Uddingston run. Someone at Bath Street Head Office must have forgotten that Parkhead Depot was perilously positioned between the great Beardmore Steelworks and the equally vast Clyde Bridge Steel Complex. I suppose they said in Parkhead Depot – "Never look a gift Coronation in the contacts box"... Inevitably the day came when the LMS Coronation from the South made an unauthorised stop in Uddingston station itself – Uddingston Central by then, I think. Much delighted, I airted rapidly yont and made an also unauthorised exit, full of joy at being able to travel in to Parkhead on one of my much-loved trams on my favourite route instead of coming out from the city up the Gallowgate on one as was the more normal thing.

MISTER! YOUR CAR HAS WENT!

It was not unusual for GCT crews to use their lying-time at Uddingston terminus for savouring the delights of Tunnock's celebrated tea-rooms. Unfortunately some motormen tended to be careless and depended in air-brake days on the air-brake keeping the Standard car standing in place outside the tea-rooms, and did not bother to apply the hand-brake as they should have done. When the big Coronations arrived in service, several motormen were to regret not remembering what they had been taught in training school. The air leaked off on a Coronation more quickly than on a Standard and several times a Coronation took off on its own downhill from Uddingston towards Glasgow. The word soon got around.

MOLLER'S EMPIRE

Lanarkshire Tramway Company arrived from Hamilton to the other side of Uddingston Cross, exactly two years later than GCT's Uddingston arrival. For a time, passengers on the Hamilton/Uddingston LTC section were not carried on the tremendously steep and curved hill between Bothwell Bridge and Bothwell Village. Master Baker Tunnock had laid the last granite sets for the Glasgow tracks and duly repeated the feat for LTC. A brass plate in the roadway at Uddingston Cross for long commemorated the two ceremonies. GCT and LTC connected by a caramel wafer?

Unfortunately that was to be the only connection in Uddingston between the two systems. For some curious

20

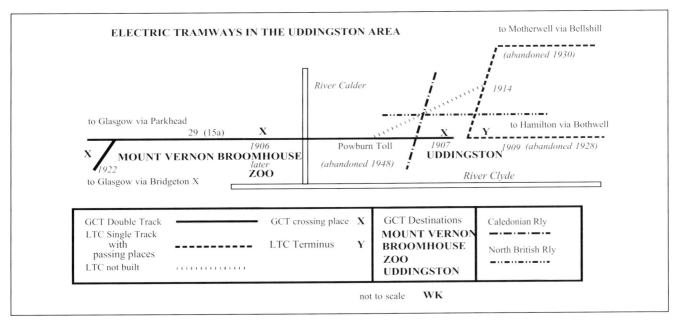

ELECTRIC TRAMWAYS IN THE UDDINGSTON AREA

GCT Double Track	————————	GCT crossing place **X**	GCT Destinations	Caledonian Rly
LTC Single Track with passing places	- - - - - - - -	LTC Terminus **Y**	**MOUNT VERNON BROOMHOUSE ZOO UDDINGSTON**	—·—·—·—
LTC not built	··············			North British Rly
				—··—··—··

not to scale **WK**

reason (LTC always harbouring ambitions to run through to Glesca) LTC and GCT overheads were not compatible, LTC trolleys being side-running as opposed to GCT centre pole operation. Later, in 1914, track and overhead came down the old coal road from Bellshill and double track came round Uddingston Cross to link with LTC's original terminus. As a wee boy I stood on the middle of Uddingston Cross (one wouldn't do that to-day) looking at the trackwork there. A couple of points dropped in and our beloved caurs could have reached Hamilton and Motherwell et al. But Alas! The last Uddingston /Motherwell via Bellshill tram had run in the previous year (1931). Peculiarly enough, I was eventually to enjoy a wee hurl on genuine LTC rails and sit on genuine LTC upper-deck seats. The aforementioned cricket club's ground in Bothwell Castle Policies suffered badly in the Thirties from the great West of Scotland malaise – subsidence caused by coal mining. An expensive new cricket pavilion was consequently in great danger of literal terminal decline.

A brilliant solution was found to the problem. The pavilion was mounted on ex-LTC tram rail and moved about according to inclination. The top-deck tram seats were arranged round the cricket-field boundary for better spectator comfort. And for a time the seat backs could be reversed. Don't think I did not do that more than a few times.

CONFUSION REIGNED

Recently, an even more aged resident of Uddingston than myself recounted how, in his teens, he had watched in fascination as a Glasgow motorman, not realising that he had reached the end of his bit of line, put on power to travel across Uddingston Cross. That poor motorman confessed that he had become confused by seeing a tram car coming down Bothwell Road towards him and thought he should be onward proceeding, never heeding! My informant said that there was quite a long-drawn-out hullabaloo in the procedure to restore the Glasgow Standard to its rightful

track. One of the problems was that the Glasgow trolley-pole had gotten itself well and truly encumbered with Lanarkshire overhead. What a happenstance to witness – though I know from experience that Glasgow caurs were forever overshooting end-of-track. The errant Glasgow tram had gone so far over the gap between the two systems that it was found easier to re-rail it on the Lanarkshire track. The LTC Duty Inspector at Uddingston then had the Glasgow car taken to Motherwell's Traction House Depot where it was checked over for damage before being returned to Glasgow. Another 'Villager' has memories of an early-phase Glasgow passenger tram being deliberately manhandled across the gap between the two systems and being driven off on the Lanarkshire Company's side. He said that grooves were chiselled on the intervening setts to assist the process. Apparently there had been a shortage of available trams for the Lanarkshire Company and they had borrowed six from Glasgow. (What if the above-mentioned unfortunate Glasgow motorman had actually seen a Glasgow Standard in all its glory on the other side of the gap?).

There had been a physical connection between the two systems at Cambuslang until the Lanarkshire company had given up on its Cambuslang service, but apparently the transferred cars could not reach Lanarkshire's Motherwell Power House Depot that way because of low bridges on the Cambuslang route.

LOST DIAMONDS

When the Motherwell, Newarthill, Bellshill, Uddingston line was completed, a service operated from Holytown, to Larkhall, some 12 miles of a great semi-circle which took in Mossend, Bellshill, Uddingston, Bothwell, and Hamilton. A great trip to be had for eight old pennies, but did any one other than the crews ever do it? (And it was also possible to travel from Newmains or Larkhall to Loch Lomond by tram!) Today Strathcyde Passenger Transport is thinking about spending millions of pounds restoring a rail link to Larkhall from Hamilton, Gosh! What the politicians and bus and private car lobbies destroyed in the West of Scotland.

ROUND AND ROUND WE GO

Eventually, because of punctuality difficulties, Holytown to Bellshill became a shuttle service again and Larkhall to Hamilton extended to Uddingston in rush hours only. The main LTC Uddingston service was provided by circular service running from Uddingston to Uddingston via Bothwell, Hamilton, Motherwell, Newarthill, Mossend, and Bellshill in both directions. At peak times 58 trams were out on the Uddingston Circle service. On the old NB Uddingston Hamilton line over fifty mineral trains alone were daily on the railway. So the Uddingston area was great for a rail buff. Owing to unbridled bus competition, sadly, the last Uddingston to Hamilton service car operated in October 1930, and most of a very well-run and maintained tramway system operated no more.

A replica Lanarkshire car operates at Summerlee Heritage Centre in Coatbridge.

MEMORIALS

To-day, amazingly, a large number of the tall, graceful and finial topped LTC Traction poles are still extant between Uddingston Cross and Bothwell Bridge. They perform the more humdrum but still useful task of acting as street light-

Carol Ann and Liza, with the author operating Lanarkshire replica tram 53 at the Miner's Cottages, Summerlee Heritage Centre.

ing standards – and have provided ninety years of great value for money. Apparently they were concrete-filled at one time to provide greater pole strength. Bothwell Road continues to be higher on the side where the LCT track ran. At the site of the old LTC Uddingston terminus, the still high pavement edge takes the odd revenge on the unwary parking motorist. GCT kept serving The Village with trams until a rates dispute with Lanarkshire County Council led to the abandonment of the full Glasgow – Uddingston route in 1948. There were also foundation problems on the A74 between Powburn Toll and Broomhouse, for the road had been laid out over vast quantities of sand. Well, these were the official reasons given, but as events were to prove, the 'powers-that-were' short-sightedly wanted to wash their hands of tramway operation.

STOP AND DELIVER

It was on this bit of road approaching Broomhouse from Uddingston through the dark countryside on an open-top Standard in the 'twenties that a friend who was a passenger on the tram warned my father – the tram's Conductor – that two men on the top deck were planning to assault my father, cut the straps on his cash-bag and make off with the takings. This would have had serious consequences in more than one way, for loss of the takings might have been deemed a dismissable offence. And this was a time of great unemployment. My father's friend was one Gerry Reynolds – once a redoubtable Celtic full-back of the Pierce/Hunter/Styles school of mayhem, of whom it was said that he could head the old heavy leather ball further than most players could kick it. The motorman, Tommy Murphy, was also a family friend (in those days, regrettably, but for obvious reasons, usually, Catholic was teamed with Catholic and Protestant with Protestant when making up regular GCT tram crews). Accordingly a plot was also laid downstairs. The tramcar was suddenly pulled up and braked. The motorman advanced up the front stairs wielding his massive, long point iron, while GR and dad came up the back stairs at the same time. The would-be villains took one look at what was about to befall them and dreeped over the side of the open-top Standard, quickly disappearing into the darkness of the unlit countryside. Cash and job saved. The goodies had won.

THE ROT SETS IN

In 1948, the 29 service – as Uddingston's GCT service had become under F-tzp-yn- (from Maryhill once more, though by a different city route via Hope Street and Central Station) – as mentioned above was cut back to go only South to Broomhouse, to permit Glasgow weans to continue visiting the nascent Broomhouse Zoo. The lifted rails from Broomhouse to Uddingston were relaid on Great Western Boulevard and so extended the trams on service 30 from Knightswood to the Forth & Clyde Canal Bridge at Blairdardie. A replacement unsuccessful GCT bus service 38 ran for a while from Uddingston to Carlton Place in the city.

Dennistoun's Standard 12 on Springfield Road at Parkhead X at the more often used Parkhead cross-over. *(see page 24)*

MORE MEMORIALS

Today a few GCT roses still bloom on building walls in Uddingston, and on a wet night, standing at Uddingston Cross, the outline of the GCT trackbed can be seen (rails are still buried in Main Street) heading down the A74(!) towards what was once the Second City of the Empire and glorious Baghdad-on-the-Tramlines. (Great nostalgia!)

THOSE WERE THE DAYS MY FRIEND

At Mount Vernon Railway Bridge in Hamilton Road there was that little-used 'Y' junction with old-style pointwork. Double track (apart from a short single-stretch!) ran along London Road from Mount Vernon to Carmyle and celebrated Auchenshuggle. Repaired(?) cars might be seen belting happily along. No doubt the fitters wanted a trip in the sunshine and fresh air, and why not. On enquiry, paterfamilias rather thought that this section had been laid as unemployment relief work, with the thought that in the event of LTC trams running through to Glasgow from Uddingston, they might do so via Bridgeton Cross rather than by passing through congested Parkhead Cross. This also raises the interesting thought that there might well also have been an alternative Uddingston – Paisley route.

I often think back to the day in 1939 when we were on a Coronation Mark One – Uddingston-bound on a sunny Summer morning. I was on my favourite Coronation seat – that single one right at the front by the destination boxes. The Coronation had just been built and out-shopped from Coplawhill and was still marvellously redolent of paint, varnish and oil. I was indolently enjoying the sights and

smells. Suddenly I was startlingly awakened from my pleasant reverie by the loud command from the motorman. "You! Up there! Get down here!" My father was ex-regular KOSB and when he said "Jump!" I jumped. With great trepidation I tip-toed down the front stairs, wondering of what heinous offence I had been guilty. The conductor, the aforementioned Jimmy Kelly, was standing grinning, so I knew that things could not be that bad. "Sit down there and drive the car", came the next command. I had certainly not expected that. I was not new to motorman status as I had previously had many "goes" on Parkhead Depot lyes. But this was the real thing. So I "operated" the Coronation for the some three miles on to Uddingston. Not bad for aged ten. After the heavy Standard controllers I found the controller and brakes most responsive to the slightest touch, but I have to confess that one or two intending passengers before Uddingston had to step-to-and-fro a wee bit. To my surprise, passengers and intending passengers were full of smiles. I have always loved West of Scotland people since then, and Coronation tramcars. Happy, happy days.

But at least 1245 is still extant and, last I heard, was in Rigby Road depot in Blackpool. I am most grateful for that.

(Highly recommended reading: "Lanarkshire's Trams": edited by A.W. Brotchie and published by N B Traction, 31 Forfar Road, Dundee, DD4 7BE for Summerlee Heritage Trust and Summerlee Transport Group.)

WARTIME

Shortly after my first "go" on a Coronation, we were at a

Duke Street at Beardmore's first industrial railway level crossing. A second one was put in nearer to Parkhead Cross during the war. The first motorman is waiting to see what is coming down Shettleston Road so that the two motormen concerned can work out who should go ahead and do all the work. This was one of the places where motormen would use their fingers to indicate the minutes when they were due at the next timing point. This so offended fastidious passengers that the practice was officially condemned in a GCT Traffic Circular. Not that the motormen took much notice of that nonsense. The edict was that precedence should be taken according to service numbers – which, of course did not make allowance for a tram running late – or early!

reserve match at Celtic Park. Coming away from the game we turned into Springfield Road just as a Standard came down from Parkhead Depot to reverse on the cross-over on its way to Shettleston. It too was just ex-works and in that head-turning condition as ex-works cars could be. There was a young motorman at the front end and we swung through the Parkhead Cross junctions at a great lick and shot-off down Westmuir Street with the gears singing their familiar joyous song. But there were tin-covers on the interior lights for the date was the 2nd of September 1939, and the high glory days of the Glasgow cars were over. I often wonder if that smart young motorman survived the war?

A NEW JOURNEY

In the first year of the terrible conflict, my school in Glasgow, St. Aloysius' College, couldn't accommodate us wee yins as there was not a sufficiency of air-raid shelter places for us. Instead of travelling to Garnethill, we had to cross the city to various teachers' houses. For me this meant that instead of taking the "back-road" Knightswood car to Cambridge Street, I had to go on the "front" road via the Gallowgate to Jamaica Street where I changed on to a Shawlands-bound car in order to reach Miss Sinclair's house in the rarefied atmosphere of Strathbungo. At first this change of route depressed me no end. The Knightswood car had taken me down Shettleston Road, and through Beardmore's great steel-works – then literally going at full blast. Great battleship guns and an assortment of castings and machinery could be seen from the top-deck. There was also the fascination of seeing into the LNER's Parkhead Motive Power Shed and noting which engines

were present. Sometime wagons of coal would be climbing its tall coal-hoist. There was also the puzzle of working out the intricacies of Beardmore's industrial railway system and spotting which of its engines were shunting around it. At the intersection with Duke Street there would be a car from Parkhead waiting and a great display of finger signals between the respective motormen. I was later to learn that this practice was against the GCT rule-book as passengers often mis-understood the gestures. But it nearly always happened when two trams were converging at junctions. In truth the motormen were simply indicating at which minutes they were due at the next timing point, in this case Fleming Street, and sorting out which tram ought to have precedence. The Department were to issue a regulation that cars were to proceed according to service number order but GCT crews always ignored that sort of nonsense.

DELIGHTS OF BAGHDAD-ON-THE-CAUR-LINES

Further along there was Paton Street with its single line into Dennistoun Depot. Something was usually happening there. Sometimes a disabled car would be getting replaced or a tram would be "running-in" with the conductor holding down the bow-collector "wrong way" so to speak. Next came the excitements of the Cattle Market and Tennant's Brewery. The interest at the latter was to try and spot one of their steam-driven lorries. The Cold Store in George Street usually caused a delay with lorries reversing in and out.

Then I would try to count the statues in George Square. (Imagine my delight when I sat a worth-while school bur-

Sauchiehall Street. This is where I would board a tram for home after school, usually having taken a browse round the many attractive shops in the area. There were two adjoining tram stops here signed for different groups of services. Judging by the crowd for the 1 service car, there must have been a hold-up of some kind. Such a crowd was normal for a "Yellow Peril" stop but not for the more sedate service 1.

sary in third year and that very question arose!) Would there be a Pacific in Queen Street Station? Would there be a clear run-up Renfield Street? Then there was the man with the sandwich-board proclaiming that the end of the world was nigh. As far as my homework was concerned that was certainly the case. Genuflect to the Head Office at Bath Street en passant, but definitely do not look at the shop on the other side of Renfield Street with those horrific amputation instruments from the past. Would there be a points' boy working at Sauchiehall Street's three-way junction? So to have to travel down the Gallowgate and miss all the excitement was a come-down indeed. But then I made a great discovery. If I went further along to Bridge Street on the Paisley car before alighting I could better see the cars heading out to the

300 in Gallowgate, passing Vinegar Hill, with Camlachie LMS railway bridge in the background. Vinegar Hill was the Glasgow residential site for caravan and fair-ground people and celebrated families such as the Green family of Cinema fame, and the stage Logan (once Short!) stars lived here. Believe it or not but 300 was fitted with trafficator arms in the thirties. Early Coronations once had them too. 10th May 1960.

Experimental Car 1003 in St. Vincent Street. What might have been. One of four experimental light-weight cars, built in 1938 in an attempt to stave off politician Warren's desire to introduce trolleybuses (always unwanted and much disliked in Glasgow!) 1003 was the one of the four, which (body apart) deliberately used as many Standard equipment parts as possible, including a re-conditioned EMB truck of 1934. The War and certain politicians' determination to be rid of tramcars seem to have put an end to what might have been profitable (for passengers) experiments.

This ex-Paisley tram 17 was cut-down to single deck to become the School car training prospective GCT motormen. Students were sent to the Motor School but although trams were often available and lying unused in the depots the Union would not let them operate cars. 1017 usually functioned down the single track in Coplaw Street between Victoria Road and Cathcart Road for training purposes. It was also used as a shunter at Coplawhill Works. An attempt is being made to restore 1017 to working condition at Summerlee Heritage Centre at Coatbridge. In the picture 1017 is enjoying an outing on Mosspark Boulevard's reserved track. "The eminently sensible suggestion was made that the Bellahouston Park railings in the picture should be moved to enlose this reserved track between Dumbrek and Mosspark crossovers with a two-track shed erected beyond each crossover – so that our preserved trams could take turns at being operated between the two crossings and thus giving posterity the experience of actually riding on our cars – rather than having the old things as static exhibits gathering dust for ever in a museum. But the powers-that-were were not to be persuaded. They managed to find money to remove Bellahouston trees for the Holy Father, which was fine, but keeping our preserved trams running would have been of more lasting import for Glasgow citizens and would have helped bring more tourists to Mungo's "dear green place". *(see page 27)*

south side, and one of them was often one of the experimental lightweight cars. 1002 gave quite the quietest and smoothest ride of any car I have ever ridden on since. I was late for class on more than one occasion waiting to see if it would appear for I just loved travelling on it. Truly I believed that I was travelling on the replacement for the Standards. After the war I thought that Glasgow would be full of Coronations and Lightweights. After the war? That was to be a sad story indeed for our beloved cars.

THE MOTORWOMAN'S TALE

With the onset of World War Two, a compulsory Labour Direction Scheme was introduced in Great Britain. Accordingly, as a young girl, an Uddingston woman, Mrs Helen Lennox, was given the choice of going into a uniform-manufacturing factory or becoming a tram-conductress for Glasgow Corporation Transport Department. She thought that being on "the caurs" would be the more interesting choice. As she lived in the then recently-built housing scheme at Mosspark, this meant working out of the nearest GCT depot, Lorne School (or Govan) Depot. On early duties, to reach Lorne School, Mrs Lennox had to walk past Bellahouston Park, which was being used as a Prisoner-of-war Camp. She did not find this a very pleasant experience and was always delighted to accept lifts along Paisley Road West offered from passing Corporation Cleansing Department lorries starting their duties for the day from the Ibrox Yard. (I was amused to be able to tell her that one of the drivers could have been an uncle of mine, for whom I had had a boyish admiration for his ability to handle one of the huge battery-driven lorries!) But conducting a Glasgow car under wartime conditions proved to be both stressful and strenuous for her, and so when volunteers were requested from among conductresses to attend the G.C.T. Motor School, Mrs Lennox eagerly responded to that request. She very much enjoyed attending the Motor School and has happy memories of operating the School Car up-and-down Butterbiggins Road (sic!). (Actually it was Coplaw Street that was used for training purposes.) However she recounts with some pride that most of the other girls were found to be too nervous when operating a tram and so were failed and returned to "conducting", but she passed out in the best sense and went back to her depot, Lorne School, where, after the usual spell on the front platform with a regular motorman standing by, she qualified for solo tram operating.

Our friend recounts that most of her "driving" time was involved with operating "specials", and being based in Govan, these were mainly concerned with dock and shipyard needs. She says, surprisingly perhaps, that motorwomen were not allowed to use the handbrake, and still vividly remembers entering the down gradient of Linthouse siding and finding that the airbrake had failed. With a chuckle, she said that she had no hesitation in ignoring the rule and pulled on the handbrake – an action that stopped the car before the end of the siding and the adjacent Clyde was reached. She then commented that she

First World War Conductress. *(picture supplied by W. Guthrie)*

should just have let the "Standard" go on into the Clyde, as like most of the cars she was allowed to operate it was in a dreadful state. When I incautiously asked her why she hadn't pulled on the "maggie" in the crisis, she reminded me that in those days to operate the magnetic brake other than on the initial test, meant making a report on the reason for its use to Head Office at Bath Street. I ought to have remembered that. (The reason for a report on the use of the magnetic brake was in case of an injury claim from a passenger. And certain Glaswegians were prone to make personal injury claims – even if they had been nowhere near the tram concerned!) She commented that on one occasion a Young's 'bus had cut in front of her on Paisley Road West and she had no choice but to make an emergency magnetic brake application. She worried about how her report would be received at Bath Street in case she lost her Safe Driving bonus. But all was well and her report was accepted without adverse comment from the top brass. On the night of the Clydebank Blitz in March 1941, Helen was ordered to take her tram into Parkhead Depot and take shelter there.

She very much liked the rare occasion, when she was "on the spare" and a motorman might fail to turn up for his duty and she would enjoy taking a tram all the way out to Airdrie and back to Elderslie. After some sixty years she is still very bitter that motorwomen were not allowed to operate the then brand new Coronation cars. I incautiously admitted that I had had that wonderful experience and she rightly became almost incandescent with rage. (Lorne School Depot, being sited near the docks and ship-building yards, had been denuded of the expensive modern Coronations because of German bomber threat. This might also explain her comments about the terrible state of the "Standards" as probably the Depots filling up with transferred Coronations had seen the opportunity of getting rid of their worst cars to Lorne School!) Mrs Lennox ended her tram-operating career on the occasion of her marriage and consequent move to a Hamilton address. But she remains proud of her tram operating service that helped the Glasgow war effort, and, like me, is very sad that the faithful old "caurs" we once loved have long ceased to run in the West of Scotland.

AN UNWHOLESOME HOLE

When things got back to normal at St. Aloysius' College, I returned to travelling on the "back" road and I never saw a lightweight in the city again. (They had all been shunted off to Elderslie depot as Newlands depot staff couldn't be bothered with them.) One morning there was great confusion. Inbound, we, the passengers, were peremptorily ordered to leave the tram at the Meadowpark Street cross-over in Dennistoun. Very confused, we were shepherded by anxious officials to a Corporation 'bus ahead. Once loaded, the 'bus took us, deviating at one point via some side streets, to the North Albion Street cross-over. Here a line of trams awaited us. We debussed and I got on a tram for Cambridge Street again. For some days the confusion of

this transfer to bus took place between the two cross-overs in both directions of my journey. What had caused this bit of chaos was the fact that, one night, an old mine-shaft had opened up right in the middle of Duke Street on the steep hill at Dunchattan Street. Apparently in the then black-out conditions, the all-night car from Baillieston had only just been pulled-up in time to avoid a plunge down the re-opened shaft. Eventually temporary cross-overs were put in for the cars on either side of the hole. So the use of the Corpy buses was avoided – with passengers now merely having to walk past the obstruction. I hated that time, because I usually lost the favourite seat out in the front box of the Standard! As other holes opened-up in the east-end of Glasgow around the same time, it seemed obvious that the concussions of the various mobile anti-aircraft guns which toured the streets had caused the caps once put over abandoned mine-shafts to shift and fall into the shafts. Most of the east end of Glasgow had been built over mine-workings.

I remember that pre-war, when the road bridge over the LNER Shettleston/Hamilton line was being widened, when going to Baillieston, we had had to change trams by walking from one side of the bridge to the other, but somehow that had seemed more orderly and better arranged. I suppose that allowance should have been made for the Dunchattan Street incident being during the war and involving more trams and passengers than did Sandyhills.

TRAGEDY

When I was still a schoolboy I was reluctantly trudging up Shettleston Road going to the dreaded music lesson. A

Coronation in Baillieston Road climbing the hill to Sandyhills railway bridge on its way to the city. That re-constructed bridge is now obsolete, the Shettleston-Hamilton line being long lifted.

An ex-Liverpool car between two Coronations at Barrachnie Cross. When it was a mining village Barrachnie was known as Braehead and my father was born here. The original cross-over was on this slope and was the scene of spectacular derailments of Maximum Traction cars. The cross-over was removed up to Garrowhill in the thirties. 1167 had Klaxon horns fitted in 1939.

Corpy bus on 1 service was just pulling away from the stop going towards Sandyhills. A man made a late effort to leap from the bus and somehow managed to stumble and fall under a rear wheel and was killed a few yards from me. I was even worse than usual at the music that night.

Some years later I was on the top deck of a Standard on 15 service heading west along Argyle Street. Not having gained the favourite seat out in the front box I had had to content myself with a seat on the off-side, and I was amusing myself by watching the east-bound motormen to see if I could spot the old dad. We were in a line of cars held at the lights at the Glassford Street crossing. When the lights had changed a red car was leading the east-bound procession and as the motorman came off top series I was horrified to see a poor chap, rain-coat wide open, running off the pavement and making a race for a west-bound car ahead of us. He ran straight under the front of the red Standard as the motorman frantically braked. As usual when an accident occurred on the trams, the green staff were rushing about trying to find witnesses and, as usual, were not having much luck in their endeavours. I gave my name and address to an anxious conductor and later a police sergeant called at the house to see me. He was obviously unimpressed about my neutrality when he saw my father's GCT jacket hanging in the lobby. Although I was distressed to learn that the deceased man had left a wife and several small children, the shocked motorman had not been to blame in any way, and that had to be said.

I've often wondered since what problem must have been bothering the poor father to such an extent that he was so distracted that he missed seeing a line of oncoming trams. May he rest in peace.

JOHN TOLLAN

My father was born at Braehead, later known as Barrachnie, and later still as Garrowhill – the latter two names appearing on GCT screens. The mining village was some five miles east of Glasgow city centre. As a boy and youth he worked in the pits operating at the turn of the century in the Baillieston/Broomhouse district. To escape the horror and misery of pit life, and also the unpleasantness engendered by being one of a family of nineteen, he walked from Baillieston to Hamilton and enrolled in the 2nd Battalion of the Kings Own Scottish Borderers. My father used to tell tales of the awfulness of life in the pit, including such little matters such as lying sideways in pools of filthy water to hew coal out of a six-inch seam. To his dying day he carried a bruise on his back caused by being caught in a roof fall as a youth. His regular army service stood him in good stead in the 'twenties when he applied for a job on the cars. The GCT was then a highly disciplined organisation, and ex-regulars were accorded priority when a vacancy occurred. However, acceptance by GCT didn't mean money straight away in those days. Many weeks were spent sitting in the depot in civvies on probation to test character, and in the hope that just somehow a staff vacancy would arrive. When finally issued with uniform, and pay-earning at last, the first rung of the lad-

Standard at Paisley Cross on a short working to Hawkhead Road. Barshaw was the name used for the same cross-over at Paisley's East End. Eventually after GCT tracks reached Barshaw and joined the Paisley and District Tramways' track, it was agreed that it would make more sense if Glasgow cars would continue on into Paisley itself to Paisley Cross. They ran to a lye on the Renfrew side of the main line situated just where this picture was taken. Eventually cars from Parkhead and points further East ran on through Paisley to a central lye between the running tracks at Paisley West. When I first travelled on service 15 it went on to Ferguslie Mills and later still to Elderslie, using a cross-over short of the Depot. If it hadn't been for that low bridge at Elderslie and the unsuitability of the single line on to Kilbarchan, a through Airdrie-Johnstone-Kilbarchan run would have been a super treat. The Paisley company left the operation of its Paisley Cross-Barshaw section entirely to GCT, but in my father's early days of GCT employment, a Paisley employee would collect local fares in the section and make a note of the number of through passengers for share of the revenue purposes. The problems of through working were solved when Glasgow took over the Paisley system in 1923.

der was to be on the conductor's "spare" duty. This meant being in early morning attendance at the depot and waiting as the first cars went out, in case a regular conductor was late for duty, or was sent home for not wearing a clean shirt, being poorly shaved, or not having buttons and badges highly gleaming, or in some other way offending the depot clerk on duty. Once all the scheduled duties were properly manned, the spare crew would be sent out to the bank with the previous days takings, or just to make a special run to Queen Street or where-ever took the depot clerk's fancy. Eventually my father was teamed up on a regular basis with a motorman who was also a Catholic, probably at the latter's request.

FOREIGN TERRITORY

When my father became a regular conductor, Parkhead cars were working through to Paisley Cross over Paisley Tramways track. (GCT cars provided the main service for Paisley's posh east-end.) A Paisley Tramways conductor worked the car from Hawkhead Road and counted the passengers aboard to make sure that Company received the correct toll. If the Parkhead car was on a special working to Paisley, as often happened, a GCT inspector at Barshaw would order the car back to Parkhead Depot if that had to

be done to avoid paying the crew the little over-time that a longer journey would necessitate. However if the Parkhead crews were not in a hurry to be finished, they would re-arrange the screens once out of sight of the Barshaw inspector, and go on out to Shettleston or Tollcross in order to qualify for a bit of overtime. And who could blame them too much.

BANG WENT THE BUS

A serious problem arose for Parkhead crews when pirate buses began to take to the Glasgow-Paisley route. These would swerve in front of a tram, braking to pick-up passengers at a stop, and the GCT men would be deprived of the then little passenger-carrying bonus they might otherwise have earned. One Elderslie motorman put the controller on the power notches when this happened and succeeded mightily in wrecking a number of the flimsy buses with the massive bumper of his ex-Paisley car. He was inevitably called up to 46 Bath Street to answer for his actions, and more in sorrow than in anger, was told that the Department would have to take "steps". The motorman replied that he didn't mind at all, for he was shortly emigrating to the good old U.S. of A., and he had just wanted to get a few of the blankety-blanks before he left.

THERE GOES LANARKSHIRE

In the Twenties, the Airdrie/Coatbridge lines were joined to Glasgow tracks by means of the Private Track between Coatbridge and Baillieston, and GCT completed the doubling of the Airdrie/Coatbridge tracks, so that a comprehensive Airdrie/Paisley service could be run over twenty miles of line. Coatbridge Depot provided cars for the new great corridor of transport. My dad loved to chuckle as he described how the Coatbridge lads (from a system with no junctions!) found their way down into Glasgow, but then became completely lost with their trams ending up in all sorts of unexpected places as they tried to navigate back to "the 'brig".

Then came the mystery of the missing tram-car. How do you lose a double-deck tram? Well! Read on and find out!

HAS ANYONE SEEN WUR CAUR?

One night the last tram from Airdrie ran into Parkhead Depot and authority woke up to the fact that the penultimate car from Airdrie hadn't come in yet. The depot clerk asked the rapidly retiring crew of the last Airdrie had they seen it. When they replied in the negative he presumed that it had developed a fault and had been "run-in" to Coatbridge Depot. But when he rang through there they knew nothing of it and he got the same reply from Dennistoun Depot. It was somehow arranged that a tram from Coatbridge would go up to Airdrie and then make for Glasgow, while a Parkhead car headed out east. Both trams eventually encountered each other without the mystery of the missing tram being solved. Panic duly ensued – as they say in the best tales. Eventually daylight revealed all. The

Standard 673 at Coatbridge Depot, GCT's furthest flung out-post and smallest depot. By all accounts it was a happy enough wee place, but I for one, would not have been too enamoured of a full shift shuttling up and down between Langloan and Airdrie. But then it would have been easier than a shift on the "Yellow Peril".

Coatbridge Depot. 1162 was built in 1938 and scrapped in 1962. (W. Guthrie)

31

crew of the second-last Airdrie had been celebrating too unwisely a Celtic Old Firm victory over their Ibrox rivals. The conductor had been allowed to take over the controls, and, somewhere around Bargeddie, had taken a bend at excessive speed and landed the tram in a field. Deprived of overhead, the GCT not having planned for such an event, the tram passed the night in the field in darkness with the crew sleeping it off in peaceful and happy oblivion. I wonder what the great man said when they told him.

If they ever dared.

TIME! GENTLEMEN! PLEASE!

To run more than two minutes out of official time was a most heinous GCT offence. When caught out by official-dom, the offender faced the serious matter of a two-day suspension, which financially was no joking matter. One worthy was notorious among the time-keepers for running a bit sharpish. He arrived in-bound at the Fleming Street timing point in Duke Street to be greeted by an irate inspector who told him in no uncertain terms that he had been the recipient of many warnings and that this early arrival was once too often. The motorman expressed due indignation and contrition, took out his watch, shook it, and apologised to the Inspector for his early arrival, saying that this so-and-so watch had let him down for the last time. He thereupon marched over to the pavement and threw the offending watch over the high wall round Garroway's Chemicals yard. Seeing this dramatic proceeding, the Fleming Street inspector withdrew his suspension threat and sent the errant motorman off on his time. The scene changes to Botanic Gardens on the same day, and our bold motorman comes down Great Western Road from Anniesland – and the whole story is repeated – except that this time the "errant" watch is thrown over the railings into some bushes in the park. However this time after the car has gone on its merry way, the Botanic Gardens inspector has a think about things and goes and searches among the bushes. Of course he finds one of Woolworth's penny toy watches. What he said to the motorman on their next encounter is not recorded. But he had a sense of humour and let the perpetrator of the joke off – "for his cheek!" Smelly buses were never as much fun.

HAND-BRAKE DAYS

In his declining years the old man would complain of severe arthritis in his right arm and shoulder. Rightly, or wrongly, he put this down to his early driving stints on hand-braked cars on special-workings. On one occasion he worked a hand-braked football special from the east-end to Mount Florida for a match at Hampden Park. Sometimes on arrival at a ground on a football special the crews could nip in to see most of the match while the cars lay-over to await the final whistle. However on this occasion the order came to go over to Ibrox to await the scaling of the crowd there. Pa did not care to admit to the Inspector that he didn't know how to get from Hampden to Ibrox. So when he came to the first set of points he asked the Bobbie on points

duty which way he should go. Naturally the polis thought that the proverbial mickey was being taken...

ERRAPOLIS!

On another occasion my father narrowly escaped arrest when "delayed for ever" by an Orange Order procession passing in front of his tram, he lost his cool and drove through the march – the unforgivable act. He was stopped later by a police inspector who told him, in no uncertain terms, that his rashness had left the police escorting the Walk with a near-riot on their hands. However, my father was to make amends in later years. He received a commendation for his assistance for a policeman he had observed from his passing tram being attacked by a number of villains. Unfortunately Glasgow police had the reputation for being "anti-tram". Whether that was justified or not I cannot say at this distance of time. But I know that there was ill-feeling expressed at what was felt to be the hounding of motormen as they struggled to cope with the difficulties of the war-time black-out years. The Points policemen used to observe the practice of standing between passing Standard cars, and could manage this somewhat risky practice because of the narrowing waists of the Standard cars. However, when the officer on duty at Parkhead Cross tried this as two Coronations passed each other, he came "spinning out like a peerie" to land sprawling on the granite sets in front of the crews waiting to change-over cars.

Great hilarity duly ensued – to put it mildly.

WHO SAID TRAMS WERE SLOW?

Recently statistical investigations purport to reveal that Dunfermline had the fastest tram service in the UK. Read on! Parkhead Depot (with Partick and Dennistoun) worked the Knightswood/Springfield Road service and its many short workings. At one time part of Springfield Road was single line between London Road to Dalmarnock Road. Eventually the eastern outer terminus became Dalmarnock (at the power station almost at Dalmarnock Bridge), and for a time, Parkhead cars worked further beyond Dalmarnock right through to Cambuslang. The point of all this is that on one occasion father came home full of the joys, because he had overtaken The Coronation Scot, no less, in Cambuslang. There was a severe slack on the LMS main Glasgow/London line at a point in Cambuslang parallel to the main road, so I suppose that the feat was just possible, and was certainly not one that many motormen drivers could claim to have achieved.

MOTORMEN FACED DANGER

On another occasion father was working east with a Standard, and while traversing the Duke Street/High Street crossing, a heavy timber dray pulled by six Clydesdales bolted out of control coming down "the Bell of the Brae". They plunged across in front of my father's Standard and ran into the side of a Coronation going into the city. Father ended up on the floor of his platform with a large and very

Standard 162 at Shettleston cross-over with the Co-operative Garage behind. The ex-London bus is impatient as usual. 162 has come up from Dennistoun Depot to do this short-working to Glasgow Cross. Shettleston cross-over was moved back down from the end of Shettleston at Gartocher Road to the centre of Shettleston at Chester Street, because Shettleston Road had greater breadth at that point.

messy Clydesdale on top of him. Poor old horses, but poor old motorman. This brings up the point that motormen of yore much preferred to be on the large open platform of a Standard rather than in the cramped Coronation cab with its difficulty of egress in an emergency situation. Though minor changes came to be made to the Coronation cabs, including removal of the cab doors, there were several cases in war-time when motormen were killed on Coronations when, in black-out conditions they were unfortunate enough to run into unlit or inadequately lit lorries. The general opinion was that there was more chance of getting clear of impending disaster from the open platform of a Standard.

1940

Some relief from the terrible black-out days and the terrible weather of the war years came to my father on Ne'erday 1940. He came in from work beaming and placed a bottle of whiskey on the table. To see a bottle of whiskey was a very unusual event in our house, for so many relations had been victims of the demon drink that we were deliberately over-abstemious. Apparently some naval officers had boarded his car that day and spotted his badge number 1940. They had presented dad with the bottle of whiskey in the hope that it would be a lucky co-incidence for them. I certainly hope that it was and that they managed to survive the war in good condition.

LUCK OF THE IRISH

There lived above us in Westmuir Street an Irish motorman who had a reputation for a "couldn't care less" approach to his duties. On one east-bound journey from Crookston, he was so engrossed in the racing pages that at Parkhead Cross he headed down Westmuir Street towards Shettleston, instead of along Tollcross Road as he should have gone. When the riot broke out amongst the passengers, he just calmly announced that the fool of a conductor had set the wrong destination on the screens, went on out to Shettleston, came back to Parkhead Cross on his time – and never heard another word about it! However his luck ran out on the occasion of his having to attend Bath Street to give evidence about an accident involving a preceding car. He was given a two-day suspension for not having his buttons polished.

WHAT WAS THAT?

The son of that Irishman was also a motorman and also lived up our close. I was just about to board his Shettleston-bound car one night in Argyle Street when I spotted that the old man was on the Standard immediately behind. So I did a quick shufti and was soon out in the box seat above my father. He hadn't spotted me. I know that for he must have had a very bad day and there was some rare language coming upstairs describing the blankety-blank motorman ahead who was holding him up. This was the one and only time I ever heard my father swear. This is greatly to his credit as he must have had an extensive vocabulary from his army time, but kept things under control when I was about. I disappeared quietly from that car in great incredulity and he never knew of my discovery.

SAD DAYS

A notorious football match took place in Glasgow in June 1946. A trophy called the Victory Cup – for obvious reasons – had been competed for. The final of the competition was played on a Saturday and ended in a Celtic – Rangers draw. The re-play took place at a wind-swept Hampden on a cold, wet and miserable Wednesday night. The referee was reckoned by many not to have been in the best physical condition for such an important occasion but there was no Procurator Fiscal interest in football happenings then and no TV evidence to be played over and over again. Glasgow was lucky that night. The 40,000+ non-segregated crowd didn't misbehave too much (there was a two-man pitch invasion) considering the fact that Celtic ended the match with only seven players. There I was trudging miserably home to Parkhead wearing my father's GCT heavy rubber mackintosh (clothes still being rationed!) and as I turned into Springfield Road from Dalmarnock Road, my father appeared turning his tram into Springfield Road from the Dalmarnock direction. I can still recall every minute of that journey up Springfield Road to Parkhead Cross as I stood beside my dad on the front platform bemoaning the fate of the Bhoys and giving him a blow by blow (or rather kick by kick) account of the wretched replay. GCT rules were ignored that rotten night.

One night during the war, Father had come in, or rather was brought in, covered in blood. Coming home from the Depot he had run for a car coming down Westmuir Street, but hadn't noticed a motorcar which ran him down. Whether it was coincidence or not, from then on dad's health began to deteriorate. Eventually he said that he was going to give up being a motorman, as he had taken his tram up West Nile Street by mistake instead of going up Renfield Street. Although no harm had been done, and the matter had not been brought to official notice, being very safety conscious, he had decided to finish in case something worse might happen. Nothing would persuade him to change his mind. As was usual with the old Glasgow Corporation, GCT were generous in their treatment of long-service employees when their health deteriorated, and he was offered a less onerous position. The choice given was between a job on the Underground, or of being a Regulator. He chose the latter, and the job seemed largely to consist of standing on street corners to ensure that trolley-bus drivers didn't take short-cuts across the pavements. A very sad finish for a very proud man.

ALL GOOD THINGS COME TO AN END

But there had been a day when Father came in, flung his driving gloves down on the table and announced that the cars were finished. The reason? He said that a certain individual called Fitzpayne had been appointed General Manager and HE was well-known to be anti-tram. Was dad right? Father certainly thought that some of Fitzpayne's actions were not of the best – especially the splitting of Glasgow's pride and joy, the Airdrie/Paisley service, reminiscent of what had happened in Edinburgh when their long Corstorphine/Musselburgh service had been split into two also.

Fitzpayne was known to have favoured trolley-buses in South Shields. There was also much alteration of stopping places, and many were withdrawn to the annoyance and inconvenience of passengers. Above all the coming of Fitzpayne brought the feeling that trams had had their day. And all this before the Inglis report sealed their fate. But probably Mr Fitzpayne's ideas were too advanced for the old-time tramwaymen, and as wonderful Koln is there to prove, for the short-sighted motor-loving Glasgow politician of the time.

PROBATIONARY PROBLEMS

There I was sauntering along Sauchiehall Street, admiring a smashing red-head, when I heard a voice from on high calling my name. Momentarily I thought the Deity was reading my lascivious thoughts, but eventually I spotted a kent face from Gilmorehill leaning out of the back window of a blue Standard heading for Scotstoun. He was looking fine in the dear old GCT green. "They are starting students at Bath Street!" he managed to communicate before the tram rolled out of shouting distance. Without hesitation I kept on down to GCT headquarters and offered my services to the city. When I broke the news at home it was not too well received. But by that time my parents knew they had a pretty headstrong sibling and the matter passed over with less protest than I had expected.

Since the glory days of Parkhead depot had long gone and Dennistoun offered a much more varied selection of services I opted for Paton Street. This was a bit of a misjudgement – for a number of reasons – as will be revealed. Induction to the tasks of a GCT tram conductor was very well arranged by a rather nice and kind inspector from Garrowhill. I remember at the time thinking that he was better at his task than most of the University lecturers had been. Much advice was given on how to deal with passengers, and particular emphasis was given on the need for self-protection. For example one should never assist a lady passenger to board or alight. Laying a hand on a lady was an actionable offence. The need to take protective care of one's Ultimate box and ticket rolls was stressed. If an accident occurred, try to take as many names of passengers and witnesses as possible. The usual thing was that GCT had more claims from "injured" passengers on the affected car than a fleet of Coronations could have carried. The inspector told us a cautionary tale. The great crowds using the trams after the war had led to the introduction of auxiliary conductors known colloquially as "jumpers". Jumpers operated at busy stretches where the proper conductor had trouble in managing to collect all the available fares. The department had received a number of complimentary comments about the sterling work being done by a jumper working the Trongate area. Too bad GCT didn't have such an operative. He was ex-GCT who had kept his uniform, stolen an Ultimate machine, and was most profitably issuing tickets filched from the ticket boxes of unsuspecting green staff. As it turned out, motormen were to prove the best custodians of a busy conductor's property.

There were instructions about stopping a car in emergency. I thought of the motorman who decided to pull the red handle on a Coronation while on full parallel to see what happened. What happened was that he quickly found the Labour Exchange after GCT had found a Coronation with the lower saloon looking as though a bomb had hit it. Well! An exploding contacts cabinet would have that effect. At least on a Standard the emergency valve just threw on the air. I fervently hoped if an emergency developed it would be on a Standard. The importance of pulling down the Fisher bow-collector was strongly emphasised. I decided that I was going to need two longer arms than I

possessed. A long left arm was needed too, for, on a Standard, it was the conductor's responsibility, when the tram was turning left, to be on the back platform with left arm extended. The motorman on the front platform took care of right turns with his right arm extended. We were kitted-out in uniforms at Admiral Street store. And these were of finer quality and better fitting than my old RAF issue. As well as the all-weather tunic we had a most useful lightweight summer jacket.

ROOKIE AGAIN

I duly was summoned for my first stint to Aitken Street relief point for duty on the 6 tram. In those days the 6, a "blue" route, (Dennistoun shared its working with Partick Depot), normally ran between Alexandra Park (Aitken Street) and Scotstoun, by means of Alexandra Parade, Parliamentary Road, Sauchiehall Street and Dumbarton Road, but the 6 could be extended for extras, and at the week-end, to Riddrie in one direction and Dalmuir on the other. It was the easiest-to-work route Dennistoun operat-

675 in Admiral Street. This is where the GCT clothing store was situated and crews went for uniform issue.

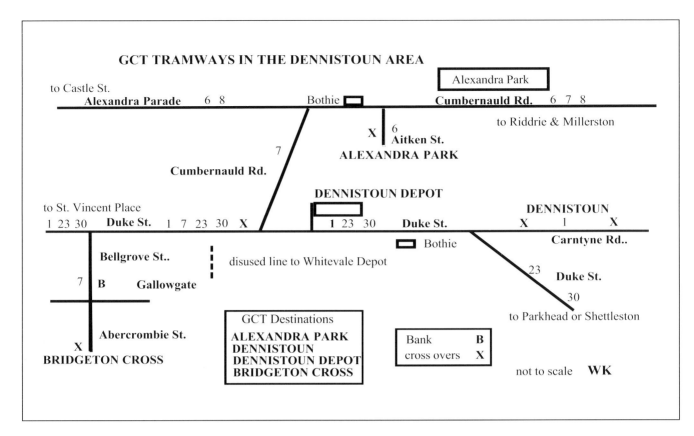

GCT TRAMWAYS IN THE DENNISTOUN AREA

to Castle St.

Alexandra Parade   6   8   Bothie   🔲   **Cumbernauld Rd.**   6   7   8

Alexandra Park

to Riddrie & Millerston

X | 6
Aitken St.

ALEXANDRA PARK

7

Cumbernauld Rd.

DENNISTOUN DEPOT

DENNISTOUN

to St. Vincent Place

1 23 30   **Duke St.**   1 7 23 30 X   **1   23   30**   **Duke St.**   X   1   X

🔲 Bothie

Carntyne Rd..

Bellgrove St..   disused line to Whitevale Depot

23   **Duke St.**

7   **B**   **Gallowgate**   30

to Parkhead or Shettleston

GCT Destinations

Abercrombie St.

X   **ALEXANDRA PARK**   Bank   **B**
BRIDGETON CROSS   **DENNISTOUN**   cross overs   **X**
DENNISTOUN DEPOT
BRIDGETON CROSS   not to scale   **WK**

ed and by far the most sedate. Obviously this was a duty chosen with care to give the probationer an easy start. Despite what I have read elsewhere, in 1950 Dennistoun Depot still had quite a selection of its 80+ Standard cars with route bands of red, yellow and blue as well as the all encroaching 'bus' green. A peculiarity of Dennistoun Depot was that when trams were entering the depot, which was done by reversing in Duke Street and running down Paton Street (usually at speed!), the bow collector was not reversed in Duke Street, but the conductor/conductress was upstairs at what had become the "front" end of the car holding the trolley rope so that the bow collector kept in the "wrong" position. This was because of the low overhead in the depot prevented the bow collector being reversed in the premises for an outward journey. On two occasions at least, I sweated overnight because I had forgotten to carry out the correct procedure for the tram being put away. And accordingly I reported for duty in the morning in fear and trepidation about the mayhem I might have caused in the depot, but I needn't have worried. Nothing seemed to have gone wrong, and nothing was ever said about my neglect. My "conducting" conductor was a super chap who couldn't have been more pleasant and helpful. The story went that he had been collecting fares on the top

A Coronation in Paton Street at the entrance to Dennistoun Depot just before closure. After the depot closed, Beatties' Bakery, seen in the background of the picture, took over the old depot. It was not unknown for the odd van to take the plunge into one of the open service pits.

Standard at Duke Street prison. This is where that unfortunate conductor was catapulted from one tram into the preceding one when they collided. The Duke Street crossing with High Street is to the left of the picture and "the unwholesome hole" was on the hill to the right. 91 was known as Baillie Dollan's car. He had suggested removal of top deck bulkheads – these being replaced with staircase partitions.

Partick's 76 in Scotstoun siding waiting to proceed to Riddrie. Scotstoun was the usual week-day western end of the once "blue" 6 service from Alexandra Park. On Sunday the 6 service would operate between Riddrie and Dalmuir West. 3rd April 1959. Note attempts to strengthen sides of this car after misguided removal of customary rubbing strakes.

A Coronation on service 8 at Alexandra Parade, with Alexandra Park Gates on the right. The crew bothie is on the far right. There is a "Tram Turning" warning sign on the left for the Alexandra Park siding. 1162 again.

deck of a Standard on the steep descent in Duke Street (once reputed to be the longest Street in Europe) from the High Street crossing going east, when for some reason his Standard had run full tilt into a stationary car in front. The poor fellow had been pitched from the top deck of his car on to the top deck of the car in front. I found this hard to believe. It would have involved passage through his car's top deck front door, front window and through the back window of the preceding car. However I heard the story from various people, so that there must have been something to it. In later years I was to discover that the most peculiar things could happen in road accidents. Perhaps a door or window was in fact open. (Great care had to be taken if a motorman practised his emergency stop shortly after leaving the depot. Most gave a warning but the odd one didn't – probably to have a laugh at the conductor's expense.)

BLUE CARS AND A BLUE NOSE

So, reporting for my first stint, in my usual bone-headed way, I took a 23 from Muiryfauld Drive to Fleming Street, and ran with the heavy Ultimate in its ticket box up and over the hill to the terminus in Aitken Street. Fit I was in those days after all that RAF PT. I was told amid great chuckles by the kind inspector and the equally affable duty conductor that I should never do that again. The tram would wait for me and such extraordinary exertion was unnecessary. Of course I should have stayed on the 23 to Cumbernauld Road and then ridden up to Alexandra Park

in comfort on a 7. I had quite forgotten that it would not have cost me anything and out of habit I had done my customary penny-pinching exercise round the Glasgow Fare Stages... Service 6 normally operated from Alexandra Park in the east to Scotstoun in the west. But on Sundays, and occasionally, it could be extended to run from Riddrie to Dalmuir West. The 6 route was to provide me with yet another of life's many humbling experiences. It was always a pleasure to have all fares collected and to be able to lounge on the back platform of a Standard watching the interesting and entertaining Glasgow scene as we rolled steadily past. Thus mis-occupied on a quiet Sunday morning as we progressed along Dumbarton Road on an extended working to Dalmuir, I began to be puzzled as great crowds of intending passengers disturbed my peaceful reverie. Eventually the old Standard was groaning with its overload and I decided to call a halt to the collection of passengers at the next stop. A few boarded, and I intercepted the rest with what I thought was a most polite statement to the effect that the tram was full, and that the rest would have to wait for the next car. As I belled the car away, a voice roared at me "You big orange b..........!" Wrong on all three counts I thought. And then the penny dropped. The crowds were intending mass-goers at Holy Redeemer, Clydebank. No wonder I never made Pope. There weren't many short workings on the 6. In the west, Kelvingrove (Radnor Street loop – was there another tram terminus with such a beautiful ballad of the same name?) –and Whiteinch might be used. (Recently at the Funeral of a University friend, the Requiem Mass was introduced by the pleasant music of the ballad Kelvingrove – which I found very moving.) Unusually on one occasion we reversed at Charing Cross. Pleasant old 6. What magnificent scenic views: Art Galleries, Kelvin Hall, Yoonie Tower, and Provanmill Gasholders!

YELLOW PERIL

If Glasgow's no. 6 tram service was rather "sedate", the same could not be said about no. 7. Even today it is still spoken of in horror as "The Yellow Peril" by former green staff who had the misfortune to work on it. Yellow had been its identification colour for the illiterates of Glasgow, and it was one of the few GTC tram routes that did not traverse the city centre. (Go on! Which were the others?) I heard only the other day from a Strathclyde bus driver that its modern replacement bus route is not much more highly regarded. Service 7 was supposed to have been one of the reasons that Dennistoun Depot had very few Coronations as it was said this type of car couldn't pass another of the same large size on some of the Jura Street curves. It was the fact that it did not serve the city centre that gave the headaches. On most GCT tram routes there was a build-up of custom city-bound from the suburbs and once that rush had subsided there was a nice breathing space until a load was picked up again in the outward-bound direction. But on "The Yellow Peril", starting from Millerston, or more usually Riddrie, a full load could be carried down to Dennistoun. There the car would largely empty and fill-up again down to Bridgeton Cross. I have many times seen a

A Standard's back platform – the Conductor's working area.

367 re-joining Cumbernauld Rd. from Smithycroft Road. It was from this starting point that Glasgow Police said a motorman had attained a speed of 60mph. Hope he had a tram with him. All a bit ridiculous of course but there had apparently been complaints from residents that this was a not unusual practice. I know we would hammer back to the depot on the last run of the day – but 60mph... St. Thomas' Catholic Church is being built. This permanent building replaced a large wooden building erected in the early Thirties as a temporary church when Carntyne was being built, but the erection of the permanent church was delayed by the second world war. The owners of this piece of ground would not sell it to the Catholic Church. But the appointed Parish Priest donned civilian clothing and bought it as a civilian. The owners were not best pleased when they discovered that they had been out-witted.

Bridgeton Cross. Turning into James Street.

7 completely empty at the old Bridgeton LNER Station only for it to fill completely again after it had traversed the Cross junctions. This load would be frantically hurled along to Gorbals and Paisley Road Toll. Then the car would largely empty and be filled again for Govan Cross. I never ever managed to have a breather on the top deck along Govan Road so as to achieve my longing to see the shipping in at the docks alongside. The whole performance would be repeated at Govan Cross for Bellahouston. After a few minutes' respite the whole business was performed in reverse eastward-bound. How I used to long for a lovely 23 run out to Airdrie! The problems were aggravated by the cramped Standards, packed with passengers, as they swayed along with the motormen frantically trying to keep

Gorbals Cross. And another heavy load to be picked up by the weary crews on "the Yellow Peril".

No. 271 in Govan Road passing the entrance shaft to the old vehicular and passenger tunnel under the Clyde, and later site of the excellent Garden festival. But why was the site not kept on and continued as a working museum tram line? Our poor preserved trams are stuck in the Glasgow Transport museum – without even a dummy overhead.

Dennistoun's 345. One of the numerous sharp bends which "the Yellow Peril" had to negotiate in the Govan area.

Standard interior, bottom saloon. What the conductor saw. Note circuit breaker on platform roof.

time. If you lagged behind the preceding tram you really had unpleasant arguments turning away would-be passengers. The mooted purchase of HR2 cars from London would have provided blessed relief had it been achieved. But would there have been a cost to pay in respect of track wear as well as the cost of fitting air-brakes. (I never could understand why London managed their cars fine without air but Glasgow apparently couldn't.)

BANGS AND BUMPS

On the 7, the conductor or conductress could collect a quite a few bruises as well as quite a few fares what with the awkward Ultimate and bag and the crowded car bouncing and swaying as the motorman fought to make time. Often in his anxiety the motorman would over-accelerate and bang would go the circuit-breaker. This could mean a struggle through the car to re-set the offending switch if had blown at the back end – though many times a knowledgeable Glaswegian would beat me to it. On one occasion we were banging along James Street on top parallel – when I was brusquely bumped into a window as I tried to issue tickets in the packed lower saloon. When I eventually managed to gather myself and the gear together, I turned to remonstrate, only to find that it was motorman Hammie Brown who had been fighting his way through the car to the rear platform – leaving the car belting along uncontrolled. Hammie had decided he wanted to sit down and his rather foolhardy expedition had the purpose of digging out the portable stool from the back of the car. This one-legged contraption fitted into a metal trap on the platform floor but

motormen were only allowed to use it two fare-stages out from the city centre. I never did work out how that particular rule was applied on a route that didn't traverse the city centre. The conductor could obviously obtain relief by having a breather on the adjacent longitudinal seats over the sand-boxes, although officially not permitted. (Conversely on an empty car, PE could be enjoyed by swinging along the handrails on the top-deck roof, swinging down the back-stair poles and then along the interior roof hand-rails. But I hardly ever managed to accomplish the feat without my feet touching the floor at some point or other. The other exercise was to attempt to traverse the top-deck saloon by hand-leverage only on the seat handles. Both practices were more difficult on a Coronation!) GCT were to issue instructions that such PT efforts were to be discontinued because of damage being caused to roofs. There must have been heavier chaps than me keeping fit. I knew a chap whose ex-RN uncle was a motorman on the Dumbarton trams. This motorman used to keep up his war-time fitness by leaving the controller on a low notch and then jogging alongside his tram. On one occasion he rather misjudged things and his car went off towards Clydebank sans motorman. On the Yellow Peril, a not unusual happening in the Govan area was to have a ned wanting to alight between stops. He would simply run quickly down stairs, knocking open the roof circuit-breaker above the platform as he came down and then run off up a side-street. Not much you could do except mutter imprecations as you reset the breaker, especially if the car was running late. However, a plus around Govan was that one or other of the electric or

42

steam industrial locomotives which used the tram track between railway mineral depot and shipyard might be encountered.

COME AWAY THE...

7 served Ibrox, home of badger and 'Gers, at the Bellahouston end, and Celtic Park at the east end. An interesting phenomenon could be observed on match days. If Rangers were at home and the conductor was a Celtic supporter the load-carrying rules were strictly applied and only the regulation six passengers were on board. Conversely a Rangers' follower would have the old Standard groaning flat down on the sole plates with passengers standing everywhere possible, including the crime of all GCT crimes – standing on the top deck. The converse, of course, applied in the converse direction. Another hazard for green staff on the 7 were "the shows" (ie fairground) held on Glasgow Green in the Summer months. Gangs of youths would have spent all their spare cash and would be showing off their fare-dodging prowess to their fair middens by trying it on with the conductor. There was a special cross-over (James Street) for shows specials – but I never happened to see it in use.

WHAT'S UP, DOC?

Change-over point for Dennistoun crews working 7 duties was at the Cumbernauld Street/Duke Street junction which was, of course, handy for the Depot, but equally for my journey to work on the 23. Unfortunately, for travel home to Westmuir Street, from Dennistoun Depot, there was no official stop at the Depot points. Since meal breaks were usually brief, especially on the more common "spread-over" shifts, time was as ever of the essence. So one day when a Sandyhills bound 1 bus slowed at the Depot entrance (as I thought to let me board), I grabbed the centre pole to swing aboard in best Burt Lancaster style. Whether the bus driver was not aware of me – or whatever was the reason – he violently accelerated as I was in mid-air. I ended up being dragged along the road with one hand trying to stop the bus and the other trying to stop the heavy Ultimate from taking a space trip. Eventually I decided it was better to save the Ultimate rather than the bus and went sprawling along the granite sets. The result was a badly wrenched back and several sleepless nights. A consequent visit to the doctor met with the "greeting" that "You tramwaymen are always wasting my time trying to swing the lead!" Did he get a red face when he discovered that in fact I was a genuine loony Yoonie student! We were to come to a more amicable relationship later when I endeavoured to impart knowledge to his son.

ON THE FRONT PLATFORM

The front platform of a Standard could carry many things for passengers – prams, bags of washing from the steamie and articles of furniture. (It was said that certain furniture firms transferred stock between branches using the trams

Millerston Terminus and a rest from the "Yellow Peril" beside St. Aloysius' College playing fields. Some days I fervently wished I was back on them. The wish was to be granted – but that is another story...

Standard 126 on service 7 in Govan Rd at Lorne School junction with loop line from Paisley Road West and Queen's Dock in the background. For a few years in the 'thirties, 126 carried a pantograph instead of the more familiar bow-collector. But GCT decided that pantographs were too much bother and expense – when the cheaper bow-collector could do the job quite well.

without a member of staff actually travelling and paying, and a cinema chain certainly transferred the big film between cinemas in this way, and a GCT circular notice warned against carrying loaded coffins. We were also not allowed to carry a person with an infectious disease. How would even a medical student know?) But when I was a boy, impatiently waiting at the Meadowpark Street stop for a tram to take me to another great excitement of life – the attempt to play football at St. Aloysius' playing field at Millerston, 7 after 7 was only going as far as Riddrie. To my amazement a black taxi turned slowly out of Meadowpark Street into Duke Street and lazily proceeded to mount the driver's platform of a city bound 30. I can still see the growing astonishment on that motorman's face as he turned to see a taxi travelling along with him on his platform.

HIMM!

One morning, on arrival at Govan Cross, we were asked by the timekeeper there to go to the next cross-over, reverse, and travel "wrong-line" down to Bellahouston. We came across the culprit that had caused our diversion. A Standard had broken an axle and was jammed on one of the sharp Jura Street bends. At Bellahouston we regained "correct" track but travelled back to Paisley Road Toll along Paisley Road West. At several stops I was kindly asked "Dae ye no know ye'r gaun the wrang way, son?" At Copland Road the motorman (Hammie Brown of blessed memory again) alighted and went over and stood with head down in the

gutter. He was wearing one of the huge and marvellous heavy rubber raincoats issued to GCT motormen. When he had reboarded, muggins expressed sympathy with his sickness, and asked if he needed any help. Hammie denied any sickness but pointed out that he was not going to miss out on a chance to pay his respects to Ibrox Stadium. I hadn't realised till then that we were both Celtic followers.

Short workings on the 7 were varied. In the east direction Alexandra Park or more normally Riddrie, were destinations used. In the other direction Bridgeton Cross (with choice of cross-overs), Paisley Road Toll, (with its interesting loop at the 12 junction), and Govan Cross could be turn-back points, and also there could be special workings off the normal route to Linthouse or Shieldhall. Lorne School Depot shared 7 duties with Dennistoun and used Cunarders – as well as Standards on the route. Lucky old them. Dennistoun never had Cunarders at all. Oh! My Yellow Peril long ago, long ago! And thankfully it was long ago.

But it did keep my weight down.

RED CARS AND A RED FACE

Dennistoun's service 8 was most interesting. Dennistoun shared it with Newlands and the occasional Possilpark car. Once officially a "red" route, its extremities were Millerston to the east and Rouken Glen on the far south-west, via Cumbernauld Road, Alexandra Parade, Parliamentary Road, Union, Jamaica and Bridge Streets, Eglinton Toll, past the car works at Coplawhill, to

Standard 154 on service 8 at Ca'dora with tower wagon crew at work. The Ca'dora was John Honeyman's 1872 attempt to replicate Venice's celebrated Golden House in Glasgow – using the then recently introduced cast-iron work. Fortunately a recent attempt has been made to restore it back to nearer its original condition. Overhead gang works on as usual on top of their tower wagon quite unconcerned by passing trams on other track.

George Street looking towards North Albion Street cross-over. Duke Street was once the longest Street in Europe before part of it was renamed George Street. Duke Street had been suggested in the 1790 era by the Carron Iron Company to improve access into Glasgow for its products.

Shawlands and then along Kilmarnock Road. So it brought Glaswegians in their thousands each year to two of the city's favourite parks, Hogganfield and the aforementioned Rouken Glen. Both parks were celebrated in Glasgow lore for having "wee oarie boats." They both had smart motor-launches also. Queen's Park, which was also passed, had wee boats too, of the scale model variety sometimes, but like Alexandra Park pond was not regarded by the cognoscenti as being in the same class as Hoggie and the Glen. The 8 service had a multiplicity of short workings. Most east-bound services only went as far as posh Riddrie while in the other direction even more posh Giffnock had its share of turn-backs. But short workings could be in any combination of these with Alexandra Park, Monkland Street/Castle Street (some screens didn't have Monkland Street and Castle Street was shown although that crossing had been removed) and North Hanover Street eastward, and southward might involve Eglinton Toll, Shawlands, Newlands, and Merrylee as destinations. In the city-centre, cross-overs in Jamaica Street, Bridge Street, St. Vincent Street, and even North Albion Street cross-over in George Street, were utilised. The latter could be exciting. On one duty using that particular crossing, the Dennistoun motor-man was supposed to reverse there, and, regaining the normal 8 route at Renfield Street, was time-tabled to return to Dennistoun Depot via Parliamentary Road and Alexandra Parade as far as Alexandra Park, reverse there down to Duke Street and reverse there again to Paton Street – where

he had to reverse yet again to gain the depot access. Ain't timetablers wonderful? Most hardy souls simply carried on up George Street and along Duke Street, to Paton Street saving half an hour and a lot of wear and tear. I suppose the fact that most trams were "green" by this time, meant that the culprit passed along quite undetected. I never picked up that anyone had been hauled over the coals for taking the shortcut. I certainly was all for it, feeling that it was a little compensation for the overwork on the "yellow peril". When turning back at Shawlands there was a choice to be made of the cross-overs in Kilmarnock Road or Pollokshaws Road, but on one occasion with Shawlands on the screen, the motorman headed on past the Kilmarnock Road crossing and sped towards Newlands. My curiosity was really aroused by this. To my delight he then proceeded via the partly single-tracked and sinuous line along Greenview Street and Coustenholme Road to Pollokshaws Road and thence back to the city. We were on a Coronation and it fairly flew up Coustenholme Road with its blind bends on the single track. Coward that I am, I got on to the bottom back step of the Coronation in readiness to bale out in case a Newlands car was doing the same speed in the opposite direction on the single line. I understand that in later years there was in fact a head-on collision on the single line, and a time and direction rule was imposed there. After all, the line was there for access to and from Newlands depot, having once served Newlands predecessor, the old Pollokshaws depot. So may be the powers that

Standard on service 8 in Smithycroft Rd. at Riddrie Knowes on service 8 short working to Giffnock. Grim Barlinnie prison in the background.

Dennistoun's 443 in Cumbernauld Road, passing the REX cinema. The REX was Charles McNair's 1931 super cinema effort which became the prototype for ABC Cinemas throughout Britain. By the time the picture was taken it had become very dilapidated and was frequented by thugs. With this and a diet of Horror films it lost its family audience. Despite attempts to revive it, it was closed and demolished in 1973.

be were remiss in not having such a rule earlier. Or may be they hadn't reckoned on mad Dennistoun crews.

STOP THAT CAUR

And I sure was "mad" early one morning. We were making our way on the first trip of the day up to Riddrie terminus from Dennistoun Depot. When we came to the traffic lights at the junction of Cumbernauld Road with Edinburgh Road, the lights were at red, and, as was sometimes the case, the action of the bow-collector skid-plate on the "lights" contactor on the overhead had not had any effect. So as we sometimes did when no traffic was coming, I jumped off the platform on to the rubber street contactor which in those days also allowed motor-traffic to change the lights. As soon as I landed on the strip the contactor did its work immediately, and the lights changed to green for the tram. The motorman – it was good old Hammie again – notched up quickly and left the scene. An open-mouthed conductor was left stranded in the middle of Cumbernauld Road. Eventually the next tram took me up to Riddrie and all was well.

Another oddity of the 8 service was that at one time, in the rush hours, a poor old red semi-high speed car from Newlands depot might be seen struggling along route 8 trying to keep up with Coronation and Cunarder, such were the crowds of passengers after the war.

ROUND AND ROUND WE GO

But we now come to the great idiosyncrasy of the 8 route. Most of the Rouken Glen duties simply paused at the park gates and carried on back to the city via Pollokshields as route 25 cars. And of course route 25 cars returned the compliment. This could fool the stranger. And it fooled many young Glaswegians too when they discovered that they were back in the city without gaining the wee oarie boats of lovely Rouken Glen. Still! They got good value for their school-holiday-any-distance-for-an-old-penny fare. Perhaps that was one of the reasons there was so little youth vandalisation in Glasgow then. They were either toiling as apprentices or riding round Glasgow on the caurs looking for wee oarie boats. I did enjoy the 8 tram service. And wee oarie boats.

25 AT 25

From Rouken Glen service 25 ran north to Bishopbriggs, via Thornliebank and Pollokshaws Road, following the 8 route to Castle Street. There it turned north up Springburn and Bishopbriggs Roads, covering much of the first GCT electric tram route ever. Springburn was still very much a railway town in those days and 25 had heavy loadings to and from St. Rollox (ex Caley & LMS), Cowlairs (ex NB & LNER) and the world-famous North British works. As with 8 it was also worked by Newlands and Possilpark Depots. Many cars turned back from Springburn, but I never remember going into infamous Colston siding between the two, although we once reversed in a complicated shunt to turn back at Keppochill Road because of some mishap. I believe that use of Colston Drive ended after a series of derailments. It was the start of a mineral line frequented by the works cars. Castle Street, North

41 at Rouken Glen. This is where service 8 cars became service 25 cars and vice-versa. And weans, and grown-up weans like me, should have alighted for the wee oarie boats. 23rd March 1959. The Standard is about to use cross-over on short working back to Springburn.

Dennistoun's Standard 17 at Pollokshaws West on short working on service 25.

Dennistoun's 832 in Eglinton St on a short working to Carnwadric, GCT's last tramway extension.

Coronation Mark One 1141 at Thornliebank which was very picturesque with a narrow main road, old houses and many lovely trees and bushes. So it was pleasant to run through Thornliebank on a quiet, sunny day. 23rd March 1959. 1141 was the prototype built in 1936 for the Coronation Mark One series. It had to be rebodied after a Newlands Depot fire in 1951.

Hanover Street, Jamaica Street, Bridge Street, Eglinton Toll, Shawlands, Pollokshaws West, Carnwadric, and Thornliebank might be involved for short-working cars on 25, but Dennistoun didn't have many of these short workings, apart from regular duties using Carnwadric and Springburn – which were quite frequent. Carnwadric was a post-war short spur built to serve a new housing scheme and was reached by means of an awkwardly laid-out junction off a railway bridge in Pollokshaws Road. This, sadly, was the last GCT extension. Pollokshaws West was once a double track siding which ended in a northerly direction – so cars starting from there did a 360 degree turn to go to the city. Later the layout was simplified to a Y stub ending in Auldhouse Road. I only went in there occasionally, and a turn-back at Thornliebank was also a rare experience. The duty change-over point for

Cumbernauld Road at Alexandra Parade. A welcome sight running back to Dennistoun Depot.

Standard at Bishopbriggs. This terminus was moved into the side street to avoid having cars waiting time blocking the main road to Kirkintilloch. Plans to extend track to Kirkintilloch never came to fruition.

Dennistoun cars on service on 25 was at Castle Street – a fair old distance away – and to reach it from Dennistoun Depot involved a complicated journey. But it has to be said that we didn't have to "changeover" at Castle Street too often. Usually change of crews was made at the Aitken Street bothie at Alexandra Park while the car was on the 8 service.

NO STOP AND ALL GO
Dennistoun had its fair share of eccentrics – apart from me. One motorman – I always admired his immaculate turn-out- would stop at every stop, "Request" as well as compulsory. This got a wee bit wearing all the way from Millerston to Bishopbriggs via the Glen – as the conductor was supposed to be on the platform at each stop. Eventually I asked him why he did it, "Keeps me from getting ahead of time", was the reply. Perhaps he had been "done" at some time under the rule that running over two minutes early meant a two-day suspension and he was getting his own back on the "Gestapo" – as all inspectors etc were collectively called. But he certainly caused a great deal of unnecessary wear and tear on each car he drove. Not to mention on the conductor. This tortoise was made up for by another motorman who also had better remain nameless. This chap had the bad habit of never actually stopping the tram if he could avoid doing so. He would drop down to a slow crawl at a stop while the passengers hopped on and off. Sounds like a tall tale really, but one Sunday I watched fascinated while this worthy succeeded in doing the whole works from Millerston to Bishopbriggs without an actual stop. Of course there was not as much road traffic in those days so he could do slow crawls up to traffic lights. Many years later I saw a Standard moving past stops in Cumbernauld Road with passengers struggling on and off. I thought "I bet it is him still at it!" And it was indeed. And another tall tale? This happened on the same part of Cumbernauld Road. One night I was startled to see the front page headline in the Evening Times. (Everyone says I'm shooting a line over this!) "Tram Driver fined for doing 60mph" The punch line was that police had set up a speed trap on the hill in Cumbernauld Road "Following complaints by local residents that such speeding was normal practice!" Well! I know we could sure rattle down that hill on the last working to the Depot. The old Standards invented rock and roll long before the Americans. But 60mph? I wonder how accurate that police evidence was? What speed would a modern radar gun have shown? The police were obviously out to make sure of their conviction. Circa 40 would be nearer the mark I reckon for a Standard downhill, and I have certainly motored behind a Cunarder that was hitting close to 45 on a straight part of Kilmarnock Road.

TOOTIN FLUTIN!
Another worthy couldn't resist exhibiting his sectarian leanings. From time to time he would beat out "The Sash" using the air-brake exhaust facility for the purpose. And of course when we ran beside an Orange band he really took off. I suppose it kept him happy. He wouldn't have been so happy had he known I was saying a prayer for peace and unity among Christians at the back.

AFTER YOU CLAUD!
"Specials" were always rather anxious to return to depot as soon as possible. One morning, at Bishopbriggs terminus, a dozen-or-so Standards were impatiently waiting to turn – and most of them were "specials". Ahead of us, a Standard moved into the near-side stub and went up to the end-of-rail to allow the following car to come in behind him and reverse out first. This the motorman on the second car refused to do – and stopped short of the crossing. A bitter altercation followed between the motormen and eventually the air was turning blue with various members of the green staff urging movement of some kind. Dalrymple must have been spinning like a "peerie". After several over-heated minutes the motorman on the first car resolved the difficulty. He shot across the crossing – to jeers from the second motorman. But when the first motorman had regained the city-bound track he and his conductor moved like greased lightning. Before the second car could get into position to use the crossing, the first car had reversed again and was now back in the end of the other stub, with the motorman grinning all over his face. There was no alternative now for the second car but to come across the crossing and go out first. I hope that the two crews were not from the same depot!

A TEMPERAMENTAL BEAUTY
Another 25 tale. While on leave from the RAF, I was waiting in Jamaica Street for a car to go to Queen's Park. Looking at the string of cars coming down from Union Street I realised that I was seeing a red double-decker of an unknown type. Wow! Naturally I waited for it to arrive, and this strange apparition was on 25 service (I hadn't seen the service numbers individually on roller blinds on the side of a GCT tram before so was quite impressed by that feature). First impression on gaining the top deck was that it was overcrowded with seats compared to the dear old Coronations. As we sped along (and speed was the word for its acceleration and progress), I became aware that this "new" car had a propensity to lean well-over to the right. I was mulling over this peculiar behaviour as we hit the reverse curves at Coplawhill Works at high speed. The car hung over even further to the right – even while we were going left – and I became truly alarmed because I was sitting on the off side. I was praying hard that there wasn't one of these strange cars doing exactly the same thing coming in the opposite direction. I must have had a good guardian angel in those days for there wasn't. I was quite relieved to alight at the famous Bluebird Cafe at Queen's Park and comfort myself with a big "slider". Of course this was my first encounter with a Coronation Mark Two, to become known as Cunarders because of their huge carrying capacity. But Cunarders were not in the Coronation

Mark One class as far as passenger comfort was concerned, despite their other fine qualities. Working the experience all out in later years I must have been fortunate in one sense in that the car must have been 1303, the only Cunarder to have operated in service in "red" as opposed to the ubiquitous bus green. The springs on the Cunarders were given the necessary attention, but although their Maley and Taunton inside-framed trucks made them splendid riders on street track, they were not quite such good performers on sleeper track, which probably explains why Dennistoun with services operating on sleeper track never had any allocated. Conversely the opposite verdict applied to the EMB bogies on the Coronation Mark One. Red tram at night – Springburn delight.

EAST-WEST HAME'S BEST

The main work done by Dennistoun Standards occurred on services 1 & 30. 1 cars operated between Dennistoun in the east and Dalmuir West of canal bridge fame to the west. 1 duties were shared with Partick with some Parkhead cars joining in too – mainly on special workings. Short workings could be westward to Dalmuir, Clydebank, Yoker, Scotstoun West, (a normal short-working), Anniesland, Kelvinside, Botanic Gardens, and St. George's Cross. In the city centre area St. Vincent Place lye was much used from the east, and on an odd occasion the two crossings further along St. Vincent Street itself. From the west occasional cars made use of North Albion Street. Of course at Dalmuir West the celebrated swing bridge over the Forth & Clyde Canal was used. (A question for your tram quiz. Where else did Glasgow caurs cross a canal? Ans. Monkland Canal in three places – at Castle Street, Riddrie and Coatbridge; and the Forth and Clyde Canal in Kilbowie Road. Unless of course you know of somewhere else?) I often wondered why the expensive Dalmuir bridge was kept in use for tram crossing; there was little track and traffic once it had been crossed. Was it simply to gain access to the sub-station sited a little past the Dalmuir West terminus? There had been some point to it when the Dumbarton trams connected at the West. What a pity Clydebank would not allow through running for the Glasgow masses to be cheaply conveyed by tram directly to Loch Lomond. I had a colleague once who told me that an uncle of his was a motorman on the Dumbarton system. He was a keep-fit

Coronation 1275 at Yoker. This car was severely damaged in the Clydebank blitz of 1940. Re-built, it was rebuilt yet again after fire damage in 1957. 2nd March 1961.

fanatic, and after surviving in the Navy during the First World War, he continued his keep-fit work in quiet periods of his tram-driving by alighting from his tram and running alongside it. One early morning he was doing this while heading for Clydebank and rather misjudged things. His tram took-off into the mist leaving him peching to catch up. Maybe Clydebank did have a through service that morning – though presumably the conductor coped with the situation.

In recent years, millions of marks have been spent in Germany building, reconditioning and upgrading tramways between the Rhur towns and cities. We had such

Dalmuir West. Forth & Clyde Canal swing bridge. Much time, effort and money was spent re-building this bridge to re-connect a few yards of GCT track from Dalmuir West cross-over, whereas agreement was never reached about re-building the bridge at Blairdardie which would have enabled track to have continued as originally intended into the vast Drumchapel post-war housing scheme (and the Clydebank/Duntocher line might also have been brought back into use).

369 at Scotstoun West. This was the usual destination for west-bound Standards on Service 1, though continuation to Yoker or Clydebank or Dalmuir or Dalmuir West was not uncommon.

an essential network linking our West of Scotland conurbations. But instead of development and upgrading, what could have been today a priceless asset, was discarded through a combination of political short-sightedness, trade-union infighting, and the influence of the combustion-engine lobby. But there you go.

PREMIER LINE

The 1 was a reasonable service to work – even when the many Clydebank shipyards "skaled". For there was a plethora of special cars to pick up the workers leaving the yards, and of course to take them there in the first place. Clydebank had a first class service from GCT. The Anniesland/Scotstoun West part of the route carried little traffic in itself and provided the conductor with a nice breather. I could never understand why the service eastward ended in the Dennistoun "lye" at Carntyne Road – which was not in fact in Dennistoun, but on territory known locally as Haghill. Maybe that was why GCT didn't use the name. (This lye had a long extension down-hill from the first cross-over towards a second cross-over nearer to Carntyne Dog Track. The general belief was this lye was the start of an extension had been planned to go along and up Carntyne Road into Carntyne itself, but I have never been able to find confirmation of that. There was one case where, out of curiosity, a motorman had taken his Standard down to reverse on the furthest crossing, only to find that for some reason the overhead there had got out of reach of the bow-collector. Panic stations. As he was on an adverse slope he was in a fix. Eventually he persuaded another

Standard to come down and tow him back to where the bow collector could pick up current again. When he was on the "spare" as a conductor, this same chap was caught in a fix. An east-bound Standard sent word ahead that it needed replacement by a more fit car at Dennistoun Depot. The depot-clerk instructed our worthy to take the replacement car up Paton Street to its junction with Duke Street. The motorman of the car to be replaced was then supposed to take the replacement out into traffic while our conductor friend was supposed to bring the defective car down the siding and into the depot. Unfortunately the duty motorman decided, for some reason, to carry on past the depot down to the Fleming Street crew change-over where he was being relieved. This meant that our conductor friend had illicitly to take the replacement Standard down to Fleming Street as well. Worse was to follow. After the faulty car had been relieved of its passengers, our worried worthy had then to take the car with its failed air-brakes up to the Dennistoun lye in Carntyne Road so that he could reverse back to Dennistoun Depot. Never having had the experience of working an electric point before, and this needed good judgement even with a working air-brake, he over-shot the points and had to work the tram sans air-brake down the very steep descent to the Shettleston Road/Duke Street junction. Here he had a bit of luck for the points were lying set for Parkhead. So he was able to make it up to Parkhead and there he reversed at the end of Duke Street and made it back to the Depot in one piece. The Depot Clerk was a very worried man when he discovered what had happened. Of course he should have taken

53

Two Standards passing on the Kingsway. The run on the Kingsway was always a pleasant (if somewhat fast!) breather – because it was a lightly loaded section.

the replacement car out himself etc and not sent out an unqualified conductor to do a driving job.) But little traffic was carried from Dennistoun itself to Carntyne Road, whereas there was a lot of traffic to Parkhead or even to the Carntyne cross-over in Shettleston Road. At both these points there was much over-crowding which could have been somewhat relieved if it had been arranged for some "Dennistoun" cars to go a wee bit further and some to have reversed in Dennistoun itself. I suppose the need was to provide for "lying time" to take place without causing obstruction to other traffic.

Later, Service 1 was re-extended to Springfield Road.

HULLO THERE!

On 1 service I had many interesting passengers, including friends and acquaintances, but two in particular were well-known at the time, actor and comedian Duncan McCrae of "wee cock sparrow" and Para Handy fame (G. Fisher isn't in the same class – sorry!), and the conductor of the National Scottish Orchestra, Colin Gibson, in tie and tails and

complete with baton case. Conductor meets conductor. But could he have belled off a Standard as well as I could have conducted the SNO?

PASSING POINTS

Service 30, was another of the reasons that Dennistoun Depot was largely Standard equipped – for 30 was a busy route and Coronations could not pass each other on the

Dennistoun's 121 in Carntyne Road. It was unusual to have a 30 service car in Dennistoun siding (which was in Haghill and not Dennistoun!). This is at the normally used top cross-over. *(see page 53)*

Dennistoun's 1088 was the highest numbered Standard and is now preserved in Glasgow Transport Museum.

Standard 344 on service 1 at George Square, followed by a Coronation on 23 and, happy days, there are other trams in George Street. The North British Hotel in the background always looked well and was a great place for staff functions etc. The building between the two Coronations and the receding bus was then The Technical College but is now part of Strathclyde University.

307 at Parkhead Cross on the very tight curve where two Coronation cars could not pass each other. 14th February 1960.

The Standard at bottom Dennistoun siding cross-over with its poor old bow collector trying in vain to reach the overhead. *(see page 53) (W. Guthrie)*

acute Duke Street bend at Parkhead Cross. (Which makes it extremely strange that the ex-Liverpool cars had only three numbers on their screens in Glasgow service: 15 & 29 – on which they did serve faithfully; and 30 where they could never have done – except on a short working short of Parkhead possibly, a working which would not have made much sense.) But when the last cars were being transferred to Dalmarnock from Dennistoun Depot at closure of the latter, the motorman of the last Coronation to leave was persuaded to travel via Parkhead and Springfield Road rather than by using the prescribed route via Bellgrove Street. So at least one Coronation made it round the offending curve. Parkhead Cross had another unusual tramway feature – a points box. From the Gallowgate direction trams could turn right into Springfield Road or more likely come straight ahead. They then had the choice of turning left into Duke Street (which was normally not done from the Gallowgate direction) or passing on past that set of points (really there for use by trams from the Springfield Road line), and then at the next points carrying on straight for Parkhead Depot, Tollcross and formerly Uddingston, or they could turn left into Westmuir Street for Shettleston and all points to Airdrie. The crossover in Springfield Road at Parkhead Cross was very much in use for cars on services 15 and 30 going to and from Parkhead Depot – so the Parkhead Cross pointsman in his box positioned between Westmuir Street and Tollcross Road had his work cut out. On one occasion he misjudged things rather. A Coronation was city-bound for the

Coronation 1161 at St. George's Cross on a short working to North Albion Street. The "skate" in the overhead is the contact to operate the Electric Point ahead. The metal arrow in the track indicated to the motorman the direction for which power should be applied when passing the overhead skate. Power not being applied would set the point for straight ahead. The two round discs in the track indicated to the motor-man where, or where not, power should, or should not be applied. *(see page 53)*

Anniesland X, but someone has forgotten to change the screens. The Standard is actually coming FROM Blairdardie.

Dalmarnock Power Station. 30's Dalmarnock Terminus was a really grim place to spend waiting time.

A Standard on service 1 in Great Western Road in front of Glasgow's first block of modern flats, Kelvin Court. Glasgow University Sports Grounds are behind on the right. Easily reached from Parkhead on service 30 – I spent too much time there playing tennis. Even after a GCT shift!

Parkhead's 166 on service 30 in Great Western Road at Kelvinside. An automatic tram turning left sign was tried on the overhead here, worked by the operation of the magnetic points.

Dennistoun's 176 in Gt. Western Road heading to Botanic Gardens past the library shop that for years pronounced itself by a shop sign to be a "Lirbary". And this next to the Yoonie. See culture...

At Knightswood cross-over. GCT's shortest regular "special" working was reckoned to be from Blairdardie down to this next cross-over at Knightswood. This had been arranged by the Parish Priest at St. Ninian's Knightswood, to take parishioners to and from Sunday Mass.

At Blairdardie Terminus. If only we had gone on from here across the Forth and Clyde Canal to Drumchapel as originally intended. If only we had kept one route at least using our modern trams and maybe bringing in the modern trams from other cities that were being abandoned. If only we had more politicians like Paddy Dollan who was a great supporter of trams and tramway people. If only Hitler had not stopped those hundreds of Coronations being built. If only...

Partick's 246 at Anniesland turning back on a short working, with a Standard on 1 Service waiting patiently to pass.

Gallowgate and he changed the points for the left turn into Springfield Road for a car turning that way. But he managed, somehow, to change the points between the Coronation's bogies. As the back bogey truck tried to head for Springfield Road while the front truck was going straight on the poor Coronation became rather confused and toppled over.

PETULANT PASSENGERS

Service 30 operated between Blairdardie in the west to industrial Dalmarnock in the east, and was worked by Parkhead and Partick cars as well as ours. At one period cars operated past Dalmarnock as far as Cambuslang itself. Dalmarnock was a real misery of a terminus. Apart being alongside the dismal wall of Dalmarnock power station there were nearly always arguments with intending passengers, (and Dalmarnock was a very tough district!) because there was a GCT rule for Dalmarnock that passengers were not allowed to board the car before it crossed over the crossing. I can only suppose that there had been an accident of some kind there in the past. For 30 cars observing their waiting time had to dodge back and forth to allow cars to and from Cambuslang and Rutherglen to pass. I don't remember such a regulation applying to other "crossings". A regular 30 short working was Knightswood to Springfield Road (Dalmarnock was just a couple of stops round the corner from this crossing). At the Springfield Road crossing trees and bushes could be seen growing out of the roofs of the decrepit old tenements. Someone once observed that Babylon had nothing on Glasgow.

As late as the thirties there was still a piece of single line in Springfield Road between London Road and Dalmarnock Road and there were no connections (as came later) into Dalmarnock Road. And of course Celtic Park was passed at the London Road crossing so the 30 could carry heavy football traffic on a Saturday. No flood-light evening matches then. Other short-workings took place between the aforementioned places and/or Anniesland, Kelvinside, Botanic Gardens, St George's Cross, St. Vincent Place, North Albion Street, and Parkhead (Duke Street crossing).

OH! MY UDDINGSTON, LONG AGO!

I found the track between Knightswood and Blairdardie rather emotive to pass over, as this stretch of reserved track had been laid using materials recovered when my favourite stretch of track between Broomhouse and Uddingston had been lifted following that post-war dispute with Lanarkshire Count Council over rating charges.

WHAT COULD HAVE BEEN

Private track (or sleeper track, or tramway only reservation) existed in fact from Anniesland along the centre of the Boulevard, to Blairdardie, while from Anniesland to Botanic Gardens much of the track was in the centre of Great Western Road on semi-reservation – very much as on Roma's "circolare" to-day. Apparently it had been the intention to carry the rails on westward along the Boulevard towards Dumbarton in order to serve the massive new housing scheme of Drumchapel and link up with the still extant tracks of service 20 Clydebank/Duntocher. That would have been a most interesting development and one wonders, had it been accomplished, would one Glasgow route at least have been preserved until the modern tramway renaissance using the latest cars in the fleet. However negotiations as to the cost of crossing the Forth and Clyde canal at Blairdardie were not successful. One cannot help wondering why it was worthwhile expensively to continue to cross the canal to no great purpose at Dalmuir but to renege on the crossing at Blairdardie which would have opened up such great possibilities. Ain't politicians wonderful?

The other great mystery to me at the time was why the dangerous double-track siding at Aitken Street (eventually the magnetic points apparatus at a lot of these junctions were changed so that trams closed the points behind them – with consequent problems for cars being towed!) which had been the cause of a good few accidents, hadn't been moved the short distance along Cumbernauld Road to the start of the New Edinburgh arterial road with its central reservation, so providing a junction for cars to operate out along the central reservation of the Edinburgh Road to Baillieston and so serving the great hous-

Dennistoun's 12 was the first Standard to be fitted with platform draught excluders. Don't think they really worked! This scene is at Blairdardie Terminus, with a helping hand making sure that the bow collector has indeed gone over properly.

ing schemes of Carntyne, Cranhill, Queenslie, Barlanark and Easterhouse as well as Garrowhill on the way. Drumchapel to Baillieston would have provided a splendid new trunk route and much of it could have been on reserved or semi-reserved track. The proposed new Glasgow light rail intended to follow some of the route and to serve Drumchapel and Easterhouse eventually! Think of all the rails, points and overhead equipment that went needlessly to scrap when their lost millions of pounds worth of value could have been utilised to lay and keep one highly modern route going at no great expenditure. In fact a reservation was made all the way from Glasgow to Edinburgh in the thirties as an unemployment relief scheme (although dual carriageway only existed then as far as Baillieston) and the pipe dream was that Glasgow and trams from the unmentionable place would meet about Broxburn. (There could not have been through running because of Glasgow's narrower gauge – though they might have fitted Leeds/Bradford special change axles.) Unfortunately the only place they did meet in numbers was in Connell's scrap-yard in Coatbridge. A Cunarder and an Edinburgh tram ran together for a too-brief time at the Glasgow Garden Festival and the Blackpool Centenary Celebrations. Maybe Glasgow's hoped-for Light Rail will reach to Edinburgh eventually, although money was not made available for the original plan – owing to the need to

Standard 373 on service 1 in Duke Street. The former LNER railway Bridge was extremely low and created havoc to the trolleys of carelessly operated cars passing underneath on the dip in the roadway at too high a speed. An LMS bridge on the old Caledonian freight relief line round the East End of Glasgow (nick-named "the switch-back") crossed high above the LNER bridge. To the right of the bridges was Beardmore's engine shed, and for long there was a store of LNER "Director" 4-4-0's to admire, so this was a great spot for rail-buffs like me. Celtic Park seems to be scaling.

get the Jubilee line to that Dome. (What that thing has to do with 2,000 years of Christianity is beyond me.)

COUGH! COUGH!

At the Parkhead end of Duke Street service 30 ran right through the massive Beardmore's Steel Works – a complex that had employed over 20,000 people during the war. Service 23 also did this along Shettleston Road. There had always been a level crossing in Duke Street just past the Shettleston Road junction to allow Beardmore's own industrial railway to cross from one part of the works to another and at the start of the Second World war a second level crossing was put in nearer to Parkhead Cross. Some wit captioned a well-known tram picture taken here as "Taking the baby for a cough in the pram". This might as well have been said about any baby in any pram in the Parkhead area in the Beardmore heyday. Another interesting feature in the Beardmore area was that Duke Street came down a rather steep hill from the city direction and dived under the low railway bridge which carried the LNER (ex NB) lines from Bellgrove and Queen Street Low Level stations towards Shettleston and Edinburgh and Hamilton. This was a very busy line in those days with light-engine movements to and from Parkhead Motive Power Depot mingling with heavy goods and passenger traffic on its four tracks. So there was always plenty of interest if I could be on the top deck at that point. Beardmore's own little engine shed could just be glimpsed while immediately above the LNER bridge was an extremely high bridge-cum-viaduct which carried the LMS (ex Caley) freight link route from Cambuslang to Springburn. (This line was known to generations of railway firemen who toiled on it as "the switch-back" – and it was planned to use part of it for the planned Glasgow Light Rail system.) I often wondered where-else trams might be seen with trains passing immediately over them at two different

levels. No doubt some reader will know! But it was a rather unusual sight. And nearby a line of stored "Director" type 4-4-0's stood for many years. Once, when working to Springfield Road, we were diverted for some reason via Glassford Street, Argyle Street and the Gallowgate to Parkhead Cross, instead of the normal George Street/Duke Street route. I had taken real care – as I thought – to advise all on board about the diversion, but as soon as we went straight on at George Square instead of making the left turn towards Queen Street station, a young boy on the car started howling his head off and just couldn't be comforted. In recent years I have worried very much about what I allowed to happen. I was relieved then when a passenger said he would see the young fellow safely home. Child abuse wasn't something that ever entered my head in those days – innocents re paedophilia that most of us were then. So service 30 served a variety of different sections of society and industry and had never a dull moment.

ALL GOOD THINGS COME TO AN END

Much my favourite GCT service was the lengthy 23. From Gairbraid Avenue in the north-west it ended up at Airdrie, about 600 feet above sea level and some 12 miles to the east of the city, passing through the busy industrial town of Coatbridge on the way. Glasgow fare-stage numbers were arranged to allow for fare-stages beyond Airdrie and it was a subject of talk before the war that GCT would go on to Clarkston. Now that would have made for an interesting service – Clarkston (Lanarkshire) to Clarkston (Renfrewshire). At least the conductor would not have had to re-set any screens! Later most journeys from the east were to be extended past Gairbraid Avenue siding to Maryhill. From Gairbraid Avenue the route followed Maryhill Road to Queen's Cross but then headed city-wards down Garscube Road. For some reason the latter was irreverently called in Glasgow patois "the Gaspipe

Coronation at Airdrie Cross. Several times it was proposed to extend tram tracks on from Airdrie to Clarkston in Lanarkshire. If this had happened there would have been the possibility of a tram service from Clarkston (Renfrewshire) to Clarkston (Lanarkshire). They would not have had to change the destination screens but intending passengers might have been confused!

One of the many low railway bridges in Coatbridge. For many years the famous Monkland and Kirkintilloch Railway crossed the main road here at "The Fountain", on the level till a bridge here re-placed the level crossing. The road had to be lowered under that bridge to permit Coronation cars to pass under. For some reason unknown to me the Maximum Traction cars (although originally built for the Airdrie-Paisley run) were not allowed under the bridge and so were banned beyond Bargeddie. A pre-First World War Act of Parliament was passed to allow Glasgow cars to run through into Coatbridge to a planned siding to be constructed to the left of the photographer. Second thoughts prevailed and Glasgow took over the profitable Airdrie/Coatbridge system instead. The Monkland Canal (crossed twice more by GCT) ran under the road here, adding to the problem of road lowering, and canal basins existed to the right behind "The Fountain".

Two Standards and a Coronation at the third Baillieston terminus. Before the war there were two cross-overs hereabouts for Baillieston terminating services. (I remember as a boy, standing open-mouthed as two motormen had a dispute about which of the crossings one of them ought to have been using.) Then these two crossings were removed and a single cross-over was put in on the reserved track to Coatbridge. When the Coatbridge service was abandoned a cross-over was put in on Baillieston Main Street again. 25th March 1959.

Road". There were two long stretches of reserved track between Baillieston and Coatbridge. By this time this reserved track was not in very good state – and the bogie Coronations were preferred to four-wheeled Standards for normal journeys between Baillieston and Coatbridge. This was the one service where one could be pretty sure to have a Coronation to work, although our Standards could, and did, rattle and sway, along the private track on special workings. The service duties were shared with Maryhill and Coatbridge Depots and there were many short workings. Almost all of these involved crossings on the eastward side of the service with Baillieston being a fairly normal destination from Gairbraid Avenue. Garrowhill (the pre-war replacement for Barrachnie) was a frequent destination too, and there were a good many to Shettleston. The latter usually came from St. Vincent Place. Only once I turned back at my own Carntyne crossing at the Shettleston Road/Westmuir Street junction. Carntyne crossing was normally only used for Beardmore's rush hour specials. (How far was Carntyne tram crossing from the 10 bus terminus of the same title?). But we did have short workings also to Bargeddie, Coatbridge (Depot) – amazingly! – as well as the Fountain cross-over usually used for "Coatbridge", Jackson Street (just past the Depot!),

Standard 310 at Garrowhill Crossover. In an attempt to halt the damaging bad practice of "cowboy" motormen hammering over this cross-over at speed, "All cars stop here" signs were erected short of the crossing on each side. These signs were supplemented with "Not for Passengers" signs underneath, but, needless to say, bad habits prevailed.

65

Coronation 1163 in Coatbridge Main Street, looking to-wards St. Patrick's Church in the background. Dennistoun Depot cars turning back on the cross-over here might show Coatbridge or Jackson Street for the same cross-over – depending on what could be found on the destination screens. This is now a Pedestrian Precinct cum Shopping centre.

Coatdyke, and Airdrie Cross. Only the fraction service, (15/23 on the screens!) Airdrie/Coatbridge locals, used Langloan – for obvious reasons. While I was stationed at RAF Kinloss, I used to catch the night Highlander from Inverness at Forres and ride it down to Coatbridge Central. When I descended down to the tramlines, almost immediately a 15/23 local service car would appear, and this last Coatbridge Depot duty being extended past Langloan would give me an exhilarating ride on a rocking and swaying Standard down to Baillieston (would the old thing stay on the rails?), where a connecting car would await to take me down to Westmuir Street. Looking back on those weekends, I just took it for granted that the LMS would deliver me on time to Coatbridge and that good old GCT would come along immediately and make its connections. No-one would be confident about making such tight connections these days.

In the Gairbraid Avenue direction there weren't many short-workings. But an odd time we turned back at the Kelvinside Avenue siding – just past Queen's Cross of Jags fame – and astonishingly we once used Dalhousie Street. The latter involved a double reversal into the old horse-depot entrance to take "lying time". We showed Normal School for that one. I was to discover to my cost that there were no other normal schools in Glasgow. At least all 11 of the educational establishments I strove in came under the extraordinary category. I remember my father talking one time of having used Dalhousie Street on a 30 working, so I felt quite chuffed at having emulated the old man. The usual 23 city centre destination from the east was the afore-

83 at Langloan where the Reserved Track from Baillieston entered Coatbridge and where the local Airdrie/Coatbridge shuttle terminated. Two curious signs were erected here. Both were double signs – one double sign said "All cars stop here" "Not for passengers from the City". The other double sign announced "All cars stop here" and "Not for passengers to and from the City".

66

mentioned St. Vincent Place lye, but on the odd occasion we might use the crossovers further up St. Vincent Street. Why this was so I cannot say!

THEN CAME THE DAWN

Our first tram out of Dennistoun Depot of a morning departed for Airdrie at 4am. As crews always were expected to report for duty 15 minutes before take-up time, and as there was no staff transport in those good old days, this meant that I had to leave Westmuir Street before 3:15am and hike along Shettleston Road and Duke Street for half-an-hour carrying the dreaded Ultimate. And I thought it of little account then, strange chap that I was. In fact I loved that duty because it meant being finished work by lunch-time and being able to go and play golf or tennis! Wish I was half as fit and able now. Dennistoun's last tram came into the depot about twenty past mid-night. And yes! On one celebrated occasion I was down for the last Dennistoun in and the first one out. Needless to say a word with the duty Depot Clerk straightened out that no-no. The first Airdrie was put on at such an unearthly hour for the purpose of taking early duties' crews to Coatbridge Depot and Baxter's bus garage, for the first local workings in the Airdrie/Coatbridge area. (I often thought about my half-hour hike!) No passengers were ever carried on the run to Coatbridge, so it was a likely chance for a go on the "haunles" – depending on the mood of the motorman. There would be an inspector awaiting us at Coatbridge Fountain to ensure fair play. But one morning on reaching the Depot I encountered an unknown motorman who was booked to take out the car. I suppose I should have refused to go out with him. He was unshaven, unwashed, dishevelled and distinctly smelling of alcohol. He told me that he had come straight from a wedding reception, and that he had just been transferred to Dennistoun Depot that week from Newlands Depot. My opinion of Newlands crews went down a few points on the Dalrymple scale. To help the motorman I tried to advise him that an inspector would be waiting for him at Coatbridge. He gruffly brushed aside my words of wisdom and said a few words to the effect that he had just been transferred into Dennistoun and didn't know the routes etc so no-one was going to do anything to HIM. I still think that the coming of such second-rate people on to the job broke my father's heart. As soon as we swung out of Paton Street, the Coronation's controller was heaved on to top parallel and it more or less stayed there – apart from passing the electric points at Carntyne Road and Shettleston Road. We were past Coatbridge Fountain long before the Inspector came into position and by my wristlet watch we took only 19 minutes to Airdrie terminus. (This might be a better GCT speed record than the motorman's on an 18 who claimed to have covered Shawfield to Charing Cross in 14minutes – following some delay to the service. He said he was a bit worried about the reverse curves at Barrowland. And I'm not surprised he was!) We must have averaged close to 30mph for the trip. We sat for about 25 minutes at Airdrie. When we came back down to the Fountain I kept well out of the way at the back of the Coronation. That Inspector must have been ex-navy, for even at that distance I could hear some words I didn't know existed till then. The gist of the explosion was that many tram and bus crews hadn't got their trams and buses out on time and industry in the area would suffer in consequence. Of course that particular ass – masquerading as motorman – couldn't have cared less. I thought of my father saying that before the war they happily used to wait at stops for regular passengers who happened to be a bit late.

HELD UP

The normal take on the first Airdrie duty was fairly modest – around £6 10s (£6.50) being the usual pay-in. But on one July day we just got stopped by the Orange Walk in the city centre, and for some reason or other when traffic started moving we were waved right through to Gairbraid Avenue by different traffic inspectors, while I could see following 23s being turned back at various cross-overs as timekeepers struggled to get services back to some kind of normality. As we were the first car to appear for almost two hours, we were swamped with passengers, and I confess that as I felt upset by the unjustified upset caused to peoples' lives by the disruption caused by the march, I broke the rules and really packed that Coronation. (Coronations could easily carry many more passengers than the union allowed to be carried). The result was that when I paid-in that afternoon I had nearer £15 than £6 to account for. But I felt I had done a wee bit to redress the balance for humanity. It also showed what a money-earner a Coronation could have been without union-enforced restrictions. On another occasion we had a Standard on a 23 short working and were halted in Renfield Street by the Walk. We stood for a long time on the down slope at the Paramount Cinema (later the Odeon) and when traffic began to move again the motorman (Yes! It was Hammie again!) found that he could not release the hand-brake. Clearly he had committed the cardinal sin of winding on the hand-brake with full air-brake applied. Several green staff (but not me – I'm a well-known cowardy-custard blanc-mange pudding – and I was well aware of what a spinning hand-brake handle could do) tried a prolonged combined operation to release the offending brake. But their long struggles availed them naught. Eventually the following Standards were somehow or other backed off our offending car, and the first of these following cars put on power and struck our car a mighty blow. You should have seen the brass handle spin then.

ODDS ON

Coming down Shettleston Road one afternoon a punter stood on the bottom step of the back platform of our 23 and rode there all the way down to Westmuir Street. He was a bookie's runner, and at each street corner, another of the firm would run over and hand him betting lines. I decided that discretion was the better part of valour. My dad said I had been very wise to take no action.

On one occasion when city-bound from Airdrie, we were

Coronation 1290 in Shettleston Road at Duke Street junction. The LNER Parkhead Railway station was on the right behind the Coronation. This station was closed when the Queen Street Low Level line was electrified. Parkhead once had three railway stations but now has none. As this ex-Beardmore's area is now the huge "The Forge" shopping centre, it is a bit of a mystery why the station has not been re-opened. 15th February 1960.

diverted at Westmuir Street junction to Parkhead Cross. There we reversed in the Gallowgate and went down Duke Street to rejoin the proper route. This was the only time I got to conduct a car in my own street.

FARE WELL!

The 23 was a lovely service and I could well-understand why my father never forgave Fitzpayne for destroying the Airdrie-Elderslie pleasure of the old days.

Sic transit gloria Glasguensis.

SPECIAL SPECIALITY

Like all GCT Depots, Dennistoun had a good number of special workings but most of them went to and from destinations normally served by the service cars and so were often not all that very interesting or unusual. The pain was that, if landed with a special duty, it invariably meant a nasty "spread-over" shift. A GCT "spread-over" shift did not involve too much hard work nor long hours, but meant that you did about two hours on duty in each of the then three Glasgow rush hours. Transport being so cheap and life more leisurely then than nowadays, most people just went home for lunch. Of those Dennistoun specials that

didn't merely use Dennistoun service routes, a fair number worked to and from Shieldhall and Linthouse – mainly to serve the Clyde's south bank shipyards. But since they followed the "yellow peril" service as far as Govan, they were well patronised by other parts of the city and were very profitable. One that certainly was a waste of time was a special working which went in the very early morning from Dennistoun via service 30 to Dalmarnock and then ran on along the old extension of 30 to Cambuslang. This was a most peculiar terminus with very little track extant beyond the cross-over, so that Coronations had to be carefully handled when reversing there on a severe gradient so their use was avoided on service 17 which served Cambuslang. I suppose the poor lay-out was a throwback to the days of the single line connection to the Lanarkshire Company's system. Another Cambuslang idiosyncrasy was that on our Coronation screens was the destination "Ardoch Grove". I gathered that although the rail crossover was installed at Ardoch Grove (on the Glasgow side of Cambuslang), the necessary overhead connection was never installed, and so the crossing was eventually removed without having been used. From Cambuslang the peculiar Dennistoun special then operated to Clydebank via Dalmarnock Road, Argyle Street and Dumbarton Road. I don't know why the special was routed that way as it was unusual to carry a passenger at all on the journey, what with all the normal service cars and other specials heading in the same direction. At least it was out of the beaten track and let me see that the Argyle Street tree was still there. We came back quietly too to Dennistoun via service 1 way. But on one sad occasion there was an "incident" after picking up at John Brown's yard. A common Glasgow practice was to say to the conductor "Three!" You then had to guess whether the "Three!" meant "A Threepenny (3d) Ticket" or in common parlance "a Thruppenny One", or whether a "Three Halfpenny (one and a half old pennies!) Ticket" (commonly a "Threehappeny One"). On this morning a work-worn chap muttered "Three". Since we were a "special", I thought he would be going a fair distance and dialled a "Threepenny" and gave change for that ticket. (I had a TIM machine that morning for some reason I've forgotten.) Enraged he shouted something rude and wrongly described my ancestry. Unfortunately I was trying to keep my cool and merely said politely "OK!" and turned to go down stairs to get the-wrongly-issued ticket forms that were kept in a slot on the platform roof. The irate bloke misunderstood what was happening, so he spun me round and thumped me one. I went through to the motorman and asked him to stop at the first policeman so that I could report the assault. However the motorman wasn't having that, and said that he had no wish to be pulled off the car some dark night and get battered. I was astonished at my dad's reaction when I incautiously told him what had happened. He said that I should watch for the offender coming on the car again and then when he was standing waiting to alight I should kick him off the moving car. This was an aspect of the old man's outlook I hadn't suspected he had. Fortunately I never did come across the pugilist again, so I wasn't put to the test. Mind you, since that time there have been many people who equally would have loved to have thumped me. And there have been many people since that I would have loved to kick off a moving car. But I better not name names.

The incident couldn't have happened with modern OMO, although there is a recent Clydebank story to the effect that a driver of an OMO bus was asked for a 60p ticket by an elderly lady passenger. He asked her where she was going. The reply came back that it was none of his business. The driver patiently explained that it was his computer that issued the ticket and that it had to be told where the passenger was going. To the amusement of other passengers she leant forward to the machine and informed it that she was going to the chemist for her prescription. A much happier Clydebank incident than mine.

MORE SPECIALS

A happier memory of "specials" in those days was that the gang used to have a Canasta School going at Arundel Drive at Batttefield. Who remembers Canasta now? But it was a big craze then in pre-television times. There was a Langside Depot car which came to Shettleston in the evening rush and then returned to Battlefield via Duke Street, St Vincent Street, King George the Fifth Bridge and Commerce Street. So it was very handy. It gave an unusual ride and saved a fare. Talking to a conductor, I gathered it was a "staff" car from Coplawhill Works to Shettleston. Often it would be a Standard fitted with an EMB swing-axle truck too, another interesting experience. This truck gave a pleasant ride, but then the tram was always cruising along with few passengers. Another tempting special used to work down Westmuir Street on a Saturday morning. It was a Maximum Traction car heading for Bargeddie. I think Kilmarnock bogies were barred by this time from Coatbridge because of the lowering of the main road near the Fountain to allow Coronations under a railway bridge. Since this dramatic dip in the track was followed by steep ascent to cross the adjacent Monkland Canal. There apparently was a danger of "life-guard" fouling – or worse. The car would be one of two Parkhead had at one time just for such special heavily loaded runs – I think at this distance they would be 1100 (before alteration) and this one would be 1106. Unfortunately I was involved in running school football teams and kept putting off the mouth-watering trip until it was too late to do it.

Another special I should have had a journey on, but didn't, was after we moved home to Garrowhill. In the evening rush there was a car that used to turn there to return home to Newlands Depot.

It was at Barrachnie one morning I got the shock of my life as I came down Garrowhill Drive. Standing at the lights was a wondrous sight – a Standard resplendent in 'thirties glory. Since the year was now '61, I was sure I was hallucinating. But of course it was 488 which had been readied for its deserved rest in a Paris Museum but had been pressed into service because of the Dalmarnock Depot fire. Last I heard of 488 its exact whereabouts in Paris was uncertain. So if you ever find it please let me know.

WHAT HAPPENS NEXT?

Much the most interesting part of employment in Dennistoun Depot was being "on the spare". It was always fascinating in that on reporting for duty around seven a.m., there was no way of knowing how the rest of the day would be spent. And in the days of youth time was of little consequence. Ah! Me! The spare men waited around the depot until all scheduled duties for the day had been taken up. But of course if someone failed to sign on at his or her allotted time the spare man was allocated the duty. The real curiosity was about what was to be done if all scheduled duties were in fact taken up. And they usually were. One not unusual task then given would be to assist in the operation of removing the previous day's takings to the bank. Largely "copper", the takings were in heavy wooden boxes, so heavy in fact that one of them would take two stalwarts to lift. The boxes were loaded on to a Standard car that then took them to the accredited bank. The bank

Leaving Bargeddie towards Baillieston. 1161 was fitted with air-whistles instead of the normal gongs (as Blackpool trams are so equipped to-day) and the old man would toot cheerfully if he was taking 1161 past our house. To make sure of a more resonant "Clang" from fifty-year-old gongs, some motormen carried a rubber shoe heel with a hole in the middle. This would be inserted between the foot pedal and the platform floor. The safety barriers at Barrachnie were erected after a disastrous accident when an errant bus mowed down a tram queue causing many fatalities and serious injuries. *(see page 69)*

that Dennistoun Depot used was situated at the Gallowgate/Bellgrove Street crossing. The motorman operating the bank car from Dennistoun Depot had two choices of route on leaving Paton Street. He could take the straightforward and simple way of turning right and going along Duke Street and following the 7 service route down Bellgrove to the Gallowgate. After unloading the cash, the car would be taken down Abercrombie Street to the crossover just before the left turn into London Road for Bridgeton Cross. There it would wait for half-an-hour or so until it was thought that the bank had had sufficient time to unload and count the cash and so have the empty boxes (and the accompanying Depot Clerk!) available for return to the depot. Although apparently the simple and direct route to use, the problem was that much of the waiting time was spent dodging to and fro across Abercrombie Street cross-over in order to allow the service cars to pass by. This was a real nuisance, so most motormen preferred to turn left out of Paton Street and take Duke Street in the opposite direction to the first method of proceeding to the bank. Passing through Parkhead Cross the tram went down the Gallowgate to the Bellgrove Street crossing. When unloading had finished, the bank car carried on down the Gallowgate to Moir Street where it was reversed "wrong-way" into the Moir Street loop, and there it would wait well clear of the Moir Street cross-over. To return, the car might be reversed over the Moir Street cross-over and go

back "wrong line" into the Gallowgate, where it would be reversed yet again to go back up to Bellgrove Street and the bank. This ought to have involved resetting that facing point in the Gallowgate for "straight-on". There was a bad smash here after the war. An east-bound car failed to read that the Moir Street point had not been reset for the main line and had an almost head-on collision with a city-bound car. One of the conductresses involved in the Gallowgate collision was a Glasgow University medical student and she did great work aiding the injured.

On some systems the safety rule was that cars were not allowed to pass each other while crossing junctions. GCT had had earlier smashes involving cars not going straight on when they should have done. Perhaps the most notorious was the sad business of 1123 turning into Whiteinch siding in error while travelling at speed on Dumbarton Road. The motorman was killed when he was thrown from the platform and run over by a derailed bogie. The suggestion was that as 1123 was fitted with "weak-field" notches, the motorman's controller handle had stuck while depressed in one of the special weak-field notch positions. After the war, there was another instance at Commerce Street when a motorwoman failed to notice that the point had been left set for a curve, and took it at speed, overturning the car. So, for safety reasons, cars from the city turning back via Moir Street were meant to do so by entering Moir Street from the London Road points. The more

Moir Street, where Dennistoun Depot's bank car would wait time. Because of a serious head-on collision between two cars on the Gallowgate junction with Moir Street, cars on Glasgow Cross short-workings from the west were only allowed to enter Moir Street from London Road and leave on to the Gallowgate. A Glasgow University medical student conducting one of the cars involved in the accident did great work assisting the injured. 1005 was a frequent visitor here on a short-working 29 service from Maryhill when it was a single-ended car. This splendid car had to be taken off circular route 33 because its underfloor Vambac controller was occasionally put out of action when the road flooded beneath Bilsland Drive canal bridge. 10th May 1960.

prudent Dennistoun "bank" car motormen would simply go out of Moir Street and run down the Gallowgate to the Glasgow Cross crossing at the Trongate and reverse there and come back up the Gallowgate.

RESERVED

The "spare" duty I thoroughly enjoyed was transferring two trams from Dennistoun Depot to Coplawhill works. After the delicate job of coupling the trams together (you had to watch the fingers didn't get crushed between Glasgow's long and heavy coupling bar, the coupling "eyes" and the coupling pin!), and making sure the bow-collector of the second car was well tied down, the motor-man commanded the first of the pair of cars, while the conductor did his lord-and-master routine on the back platform of the second one. There was no instruction given as to safety, rules, or regulations, and no-one bothered that the second car's braking systems were inoperative – apart from the hand-brake that is. I sometimes wondered how I was

supposed to stop the pair of cars if mischance befell the motorman with the power "on" on the first car. But it was a lovely day's idleness having a free tour of Glasgow. The route was usually to Parkhead Cross and down the Gallowgate (a nice change!) to Argyle Street. We would then turn left at Glassford Street and run to the works through the Gorbals. Again this was "strange" territory. The return journey might involve returning two cars back to Dennistoun or might just mean a "free hurl" as a passenger. (If you were travelling as a passenger in uniform you had to vacate your seat if there was a passenger standing – which was fair enough. But that meant assisting the conductor/conductress on the back platform.)

Another interesting "chore" might mean transferring a car or cars to another depot, especially to Maryhill for some reason. Having to transfer one car was not such a bad deal, but transferring a coupled pair presented a bit of a problem. Rightly the Duty Depot Clerk would always insist that the Dennistoun Depot screens be brought back

Inside Coplawhill Works.

Maryhill Depot – this was in Celtic Street, the shortest street in Glasgow. This is where single-ender 1005 would reverse on the depot Y to return to Glasgow Cross. Doctor Who has arrived to make a phone call.

Standard 1051 Maximum Traction Car 1112 at Trongate. The Tron Steeple is a relic of the Collegiate Church of St. Mary and St. Anne burnt down by the Hellfire Club in 1793. Like the poor, hooligans are always with us. The Tron is now refurbished to modern standards as a theatre. 10th May 1960. *(see page 70)*

home from whichever depot the trams were deposited. The journey back as passenger would involve a change of car, if the "foreign" depot was not on a Dennistoun service, and struggling through busy streets with two sets of heavy screens was bad enough, but imagine having to do it with four – which was the case if two cars had been transferred and their screens had to be brought back. Desperate Glasgow humour didn't help. "Somebody stole yer caur then, son?" Bud Neil wasn't in it! But at least it was fascinating having a look inside various depots. I always thought how superior Parkhead and Newlands were to the rest we visited. Possilpark seemed so huge and yet Newlands held more cars.

AWAY AND WORK

If there was nothing else for us to do, the Depot Clerk might just suggest that we take a car out and do a run or two. (The sad thing was that there were always spare cars lying in the depot because although students had been passed through the motor school, the Union would not allow students to operate the cars.) Often we were told to go down to St. Vincent Place and report to the Inspector on duty there for further instructions as to how we could best serve the city. On one occasion the Inspector was not around so we just sat on in the lye. Eventually I was recognising crews coming past us on return trips and they were giving us some quizzical looks. I said to the motorman that this was all very boring and suggested that we might take a run to Crossstobs or Broomhouse or somewhere else unusual. But he wasn't having any of that, and correctly pointed out that his instructions were to report to the duty inspector and if that gentleman wasn't where he should have been it wasn't his problem. So we sat in St. Vincent Place for around three hours watching the passing scene and then the motorman decided, instruction or no instruction, that we were due a lunch break, so we set off for home. Not a profitable morning for the GCT as far as we were concerned.

Dennistoun's Standard 376 turning from Duke Street into Bellgrove at the old cattle market.

TRAMS COULDN'T SWIM

On another occasion with the same motorman, we had been enjoying ourselves by being paid for just sitting around in the depot bothie blethering. We should have gone and hid on one of the cars, because the Depot Clerk spotted us, and realising that he had quite forgotten about us for a couple of hours, he mused that he could not really allow ourselves to waste time quite like that, and suggested that we might like to take a car out and go to Anniesland and back. For some reason the car allocated was a "yellow" one in very nice condition. It was a Sunday and I was quite enjoying the good life as we jazzed down Duke Street. However the reverie was severely disturbed as we passed across the Bellgrove Street junction. A much disturbed motorman travelling as passenger on the platform was rather lurid in his language as he pointed out that the so-and-so at the front was going the wrong way. He took some persuading that we had Anniesland up on the screens. He was definitely not amused that Holy Day. Of course, I was remiss in not having called out at the tram stops that we were not on service 7 but service 1. As we rounded George Square, the father-and-mother of a thunder storm broke over the city centre. There was a real deluge, which suited me fine, as there were no passengers about to pick-up. The storm cleared about Botanic Gardens, but when we crossed the crest of Great Western Road past Kelvinside, the motorman pulled-up suddenly. Ahead of us Bingham's Pond wasn't in its usual place on the left of the dual-carriageway. Instead it had grown somewhat, and, trebled in size, it now extended like a new firth, right across the tram lines ahead. "Are you going to go back "wrong-line" to Kelvinside and turn?" I asked in my innocence. "Nah!" the answer came. "This is gonna be great fun!" And with that he released the brakes, worked on to top parallel, and fairly rocketed down the hill into the dip of Great Western Road, now occupied by this great mass of water. Self-preservation caused me to belt up the back stairs just as the floor-boards lifted and a huge water-fall in reverse shot out of the back of the old tram. Of course the poor thing expired at Anniesland and a friendly 24 gave us a couple down to Partick. And so I added another depot to my collection. But do you know, although I waited in great perturbation, I never heard another word from anybody about the events. But I still feel regret that that should have happened to such a nice car.

THOSE WERE THE DAYS, MY FRIEND!

Later, when life became rigid and I was following the same monotonous daily routine – I used to have great nostalgia for those Dennistoun days "on the spare" when I could always expect the unexpected!

ANY MORE FARES?

Passengers were usually just ordinary people going about their human tasks but ...

An odd few were determined to "do" the green staff – one way or another. (And it must be admitted that a few of the green staff were not honest and true by this time either: some of their dodges included not collecting fares inbound at the rush hours until the city centre was reached. They would remain on the platform under the stairs on the journey from the outer terminus. In the city as the passengers rushed off the tram to be at their work, they would hand their fare cash to the conductor/conductress saying "three" or "two" or whatever. Of course the "fiddler" would merely issue a penny ticket! Being in that tearing hurry the punter wouldn't bother to check. And a penny was useful in those days. Another "fiddle" with the Ultimate ticket machine was to tear only half the ticket off and give that to one customer and issue the remaining half to the next. Some green staff had keys for the red "honesty" boxes and could easily "beat" the security.) Many families were well known to ticket inspectors as regular fare dodgers, and you soon got to know them too. But they were never abashed when challenged. If a passenger said there was no money for a fare, the official line was that that passenger had to be carried to the intended destination regardless. An unpaid fare form had to be filled up with the passenger's name and address and an official would then call at that address to collect the unpaid fare! Sure! Many such names and addresses were fictitious. Again there were places where passengers regularly rode a stop or two beyond their proper fare stage. If in the mood, a bit of amusement could be had by asking a friendly motorman to wait at the particular fare stage and then to go round and check the tickets. OMO took a lot of fun out of life. A particular place for fare dodging was in Great Western Road at Park Road, where

Kelvingrove Underground Station was one stop past Park Road Fare Stage – going west.

A danger to be watched to prevent pay-in shortage was the practice of a passenger to hand a florin (two shillings – 20p) for a fare and then to insist that it had been half-crown (two shillings and sixpence – 25p). It may not seem much now after years of inflation but sixpence was a lot to lose in those immediate post-war days. Sometimes the crooks tried it on with a sixpence (5p), claiming it had been a shilling (10p). The precaution (taught by dad) was to keep the silver coin in the closed left hand, issue ticket and change, and then if a confrontation arose, open the fist and show the actual coin given. Another dodge they sometimes perpetrated was to offer a ten shilling (50p) or a pound note for 1d fare (240d = £1!) in the hope that the conductor/conductress couldn't take the time to give change. Boy! Were some of them disillusioned. You could give them back 239 coins – which lightened the cash bag somewhat and saved time cashing-in at the end of the duty. But usually the change given for a pound had, perforce, to include some silver – which spoiled the fun. Bag dipping was not unknown, so silver was put into a linen bag in an inside pocket, while the notes which were occasionally received were pinned to the inside of the tunic. (Another paternal precaution.) But on one occasion when I returned home to the house and hung up the tunic, there were £4 in notes pinned to the lining.

This was a good part of a week's wages. It was so unusu-

Standard 271 on service 1 in Great Western Road at Bingham's Pond where the severe flooding took place after a Sunday afternoon thunderstorm. The pond is to the right of the on-coming bus.

Jimmy the tram dog wondering why he cannot board Supertram in Sheffield and have a ride. *(W. Guthrie)*

The very last tram to leave Dennistoun Depot. This is the Coronation that rounded that forbidden Duke Street bend, so it is appropriate that it is almost displaying service number 30. In the group are the non-stop, all stop, and the flute experts. Take your pick! But aren't they all beautifully turned out for the last rites? *(W. Guthrie)*

al to have notes at all, I had completely forgotten they were there and had to make a return trip to the depot before the police knocked on the door. I was late for tennis that night, and my mother wasn't pleased at the tea being spoiled.

EXTENDED HOURS

Another hazard was the occasional drunk. And in fairness to Baghdad-on-the-Caurlines they were few and far between. But they had to be carried if they managed to pay their fare. And normally they did not bother passengers too much. Of course if they did, they had to be "put off". Sometimes when a car was left in the depot for the night there might be someone sleeping it off upstairs. What did they think when they came round? I had an acquaintance who claims that he fell asleep going home eastwards to Shettleston, woke-up at Baillieston, fell asleep again going back down, missed Shettleston again and ended up back in town. Of course by that time trams were heading for depots so he had a bit of a walk eventually, which sobered him up a wee bit. There was a famous Glasgow punter, who on a Friday night, when his local "howf" closed, (9pm closing in those days) would ascend a Kilmarnock bogie in Bridgeton complete with a "supply". He then peacefully quaffed his quota to Dalmuir West and back, bothering no-one, and tottered off home on return a happy fellow.

WATCH THE DUG, MISTER!

But the passengers I loved having were our faithful friends, and Glasgow dogs were invariably well-behaved. Used to tram travel, they knew to follow Glasgow's dictum that dogs were only allowed to travel upstairs and once on the top deck they squatted happily under the seat enjoying the company. Unfortunately there was also a rule that only one dog was allowed to travel on any one car and I never liked having to refuse an owner boarding permission because there was already a dog upstairs. We carried the professionals too, especially to and from the Carntyne track.

At least good old GCT was more generous to mutts than miserable Manchester and Sheffield are today with their total ban on our friends. Having unsuspectingly pre-bought tickets in Sheffield at Spring Lane we were turned back because of the Labrador with us. When we asked for a refund we were brusquely given the daft reply that we would have to travel to Head Office to claim a refund.

MUSTAPHA TANNER, POPPA BOBBIN & PHILLIP McCANN

Every year there was one very happy Saturday for most Glaswegians and most tram crews. On Glasgow University's Rag Day for Charities, a vast motley crowd of eedjits would ride round the city jumping on and of the trams with their collecting cans. King Farouk and Groucho Marx would be bi-locational and there were even more clowns than usual in the Glasgow streets. Until he was moved on by a good-humoured blue-coated minion of the law, one not-so-bright wight spent a happy quarter of an hour changing the points at Woodlands Road for the motor-

men misusing an ice-axe to do so. I noted that, without exception, every motorman grinned, but took jolly good care to see that the points had been properly put over. The folly of youth. I also took jolly good care not to tell the old man that one.

THE PRESENT

Thankfully one can still have the joyful experience of rides on Glasgow caurs. Happily the enthusiasts of the National Tramway Museum situated at Crich (near Matlock) in Derbyshire have saved and restored several trams that once served "the dear green place".

There is an ex-Paisley car restored to original Paisley condition and an ex-Liverpool double-decker that is back in original Liverpool livery. Crich has two Standards and Maximum Traction cars as well as a smashing Cunarder and a wonderful, wonderful Coronation – easily the most comfortable city passenger vehicle ever – not that I am biased. (Visit Crich and experience it for yourself! And there are another 40 cars to see there too) (Crich is appropriately "Cardale" of the TV series "Peak Practice) and is handily reached off the M1.)

The best time to visit the Tramway Museum is on its celebrated Tramathon Sunday, now called Tramjamboree, when all operable trams are out in service, because then you can be assured of a ride on a genuine Glesca caur during your visit. The Tramjamboree is usually held on the penultimate Sunday of May.

If you like to have a go on the "haunles" (and why not?), the wonderful people at Crich can arrange that for you also. Telephone 01773 852565.

At the moment of writing there is a Glasgow Standard in Paris and there are Coronations in Blackpool and Kennebunkport, USA.

Of course Glasgow's fine Transport Museum has an assortment of preserved trams too, but rather surprisingly it hasn't an example of a Maximum Traction car, though the "Kilmarnock Bogies" once faithfully served the Kelvin Hall where the Transport Museum is now sited. The Transport Museum haven't even bothered to put up overhead for the trams' bow-collectors. Many suggestions have been made that these static exhibits could be put to work on a local museum line and so be an even better tourist attraction for Glasgow. This happens in so many cities of the world who are also proud of their tramway heritage, but sadly that does not seem to be a practical proposition for the present powers that be. Alas!

Also two groups of Scottish tram enthusiasts, Scottish International Tramway Association and Summerlee Transport Group, have two ex-Paisley trams 1016 and 1017 which once operated in Glasgow service which they are in the process of restoring to operating and passenger-carrying condition for service at Summerlee, Coatbridge.

Some of the profits from the sale of this book will go towards the restoration of Coronation 1245.

Anyone interested in assisting in tram restoration might like to telephone 01236 431262 for further information.

LACRIMOSA

"Whaur's that caur that wance did the ton,

doon Great Western Road on the auld Yoker run?

The clippie aye kent how dae deal wi' ra nyaff.

"If yer gaun – well, come oan – if yer no' well git aff!"

I think o' the days o' ma tenement hame,

We've noo fancy hooses, but they're no jist the same.

I'll swop yer gizunders, flyovers and jams,

Fur a tuppenny ride on the auld Parkheid trams.

Anon.

TAILPIECE

DOMINUS NOBISCUM

When the late Bishop Donald Renfrew was a young assistant priest in St. Joseph's Woodside Road Parish in Glasgow, he received a Sick Call to the distant Canniesburn Hospital. In those days, priests of the Glasgow Archdiocese were not allowed to own motor-cars, and St. Joseph's parish - like so many in the city - was impoverished and had no Parish transport. Perforce Father Renfrew had to do what most Glaswegians, who had to travel, did in those days, he went down to the nearest tram-stop. There he boarded a Coronation car heading for Milngavie on Service 13.

As he settled into his seat in the downstairs saloon, the conductress approached to collect his fare. At that, the motorman applied air to the brakes and pulled the tram to a stop. He rushed through the car calling to the conductress   "Naw! Naw! He's a Faither and we don't take money frae Faithers, hen!"

"Where ye gaun, Faither?" "Canniesburn?" "Is it a Sick Call, Faither?" "Right hen. Get up the stairs and tell them up there we're no stopping till Canniesburn." "Did ye all hear that? It's a Sick Call and we're no stopping." All this despite Father Renfrew's protests. So they went pell-mell up through Maryhill with the Coronation going flat-out where possible.

Arriving at the Hospital Stop, the motorman again came through the car. "There ye are Faither. Ah did ma best and Ah hope yer no too late? If there were rails Ah'd take ye right up tae the Ward!"

And not one passenger objected.

Glaswegians were generous-hearted people in those days.

GLOSSARY

airted	departed
badger	broc (Ibrox means the home of the broc)
Baghdad-on the caur-lines	Glasgow
bhoys	the one and only Celtic Football Club
blethering	wasting time gossiping
bothie	place for rest, refreshment and recreation
breenge	make a rush
Brig	Coatbridge
Buddies	from Paisley
Killies	from Kilmarnock
Pseudo-Dunedin	aping Edinburgh
caurs	trams, tramcars
clippie	conductress
dae	do
deal	arrangement
disnae	doesn't
dreeped	dropped down
dug	canine friend
eedjits	idiots
Enniesland	Anniesland
errapolis	a member of the constabulary is approaching
fancy	like, care very much for
gaun	going
gers	Rangers Football Club or followers thereof
gizunder	underpass
Glesca	Glasgow – "the dear green place" of Mungo
hauden	holding
haunles	handles, controls
hen	Glasgow male's way of addressing a young lady he likes or respects
hoo-doo	cursed, afflicted
hoose	house
howf	pub
hurl	trip
Jimmy	any male Glaswegian was so addressed
Kailvinside	Kelvinside
kent	known
maggie	magnetic brake (sometimes "the Jimmy" in Sassenachland)
middens	Scots' comedians' way of kidding about maidens, young girls
ned	disagreeable male, pain in the neck
Ne'erday	New Year's Day
nippy	smart
nyaff	pain in the neck, pest
oan	on
Palais	Dance hall
peching	out of breath
peerie	a spinning top
ra	the

ra thing	just the job, all right, splendid
Saxby	manufacturer of tramway equipment
scaling	coming out
sheddens	road junction
shimmy	dancing
shufti	look round, inspection
skaled	came out, emptied
slider	large ice-cream wafer
staunen	standing
steamie	public wash house
tae	to
tooting flutin	playing the flute
weans	children
whaur	where
wi', wie	with
wight	simpleton
wiz	was
wur	our
ye	you
yins	ones
yont	away
Yoonie	University

TRANSLATIONS OF SOME GCT DESTINATION NAMES
(authorities often differ!)

Airdrie	high hill pasture
Auchenshuggle	field of the barley
Barrhead	top head
Battlefield	site of battle of Langside
Bellahouston	village with crucifix
Bishopriggs	bridge of the Bishop of Glasgow
Cambuslang	creek of the ship
Carmyle	bare rock
Clarkston	village of the cleric
Coatbridge	bridge by the wood
Crookston	named after the Norman Robert de Croc
Dalmarnock	field of St. Marnock
Dalmuir	big field
Dennistoun	Daniel's town
Giffnock	little ridge
Govan	little hill
Ibrox	home of the broc (badger)
Milngavie	windmill
Mount Vernon	George Washington's estate in Vermont
Nitshill	little hill with the nuts
Paisley	pasture slope
Pollokshaws	little pool in the woods
Renfrew	point of the current
Riddrie	red shieling
Rutherglen	red valley
Shettleston	village at the cross-roads
Uddingston	village of Oda

If anyone has other translations I would be grateful to know.

79

EXTRACTS FROM GCT TRAFFIC CIRCULARS

No. 28 20/10/46

11. Reports are being received that motormen driving "Coronation" type trams are, when late, proceeding to and from Parkhead via Duke Street instead of via Gallowgate. This is a dangerous practice, and the instructions imparted at the Motor School are repeated – "In no circumstances may Remote Control ("Coronation") type trams be allowed to proceed to or from Parkhead Cross via Duke Street."

As a native of Parkhead I never saw such interesting events (and it would have been more than interesting if someone was doing this in the opposite direction!), though the last Coronation to leave Dennistoun Depot was deliberately taken round this way en route to Dalmarnock Depot.

What is puzzling though is what duties the offending "remote controlled cars" were coming off that would take them via Duke St. to Parkhead. Has anyone any ideas?

No.38 9/2/47

13. A new type of British Standard Fire Hydrant is being installed in the city. In the new type the outlet is similar but the valve opens in the reverse direction to the old plug type. Employees who may have occasion to use fire hydrants must observe great care before drawing water, and should note that on no account should the spindle of the new type be struck a sharp blow with the key or any other instrument, as this renders the hydrant useless.

The mind boggles!

No.45 18/5/47

3. A new type of caution sign has been installed in Great Western Road at Hyndland Road. The sign is suspended from the span wire over the track from the city, and reads "Caution – Trams turning left". The sign is lit in conjunction with operation of the electric points leading into Hyndland Road, and is switched off by a contactor after the trams have negotiated the corner. Drivers are asked to exercise care when approaching this point, and conductors are notified that they must be on the rear platform to give hand signals to oncoming traffic.

When did this signal go out of use? Were there any other such installations in Glasgow or elsewhere in the UK? One can imagine some of the hand signals that might have been given!

No.49 13/7/47

5. "The following notice issued on 31st July, 1925, and re-issued on 8th January, 1943, and 31st May, 1944, is again brought to the notice of motormen and conductors:-

"The General Manager has made arrangements with the Secretary, the General Post Office, Edinburgh, by which, on occasion, mail may be carried on the front platform of any tramcar from the railway station at Coatbridge to the Post office at Airdrie.

The mail will be put on the front platform by a Post Office official, and will be removed from the car by an official from Airdrie.

No charge is made for this service, and the Post Office accepts all responsibility."

This raises several questions! What happened if the car was a Coronation and what if the official did not meet the tram at Airdrie? Does anyone know when the privilege ended? I worked on the 23 service and never saw it happen.

No. 71 16/5/48

4. Some members of the operating staff due to surrender clothing for the above year have so far failed to do so. Attention is drawn to separate lists of badge numbers posted in all Depots and Garages on 23rd February, showing the numbers of coupons due to be surrendered. No summer, or further issue of uniform will be made to any employee who is in arrears.

9. Intimation has been received by the Department that Alarm Clocks are now available from a city firm at a cost of 25s. 6d. (£1:27,1/2p) each. The name of the firm may be had on application to the Personnel Department, 45 Bath St.

Thank you Sir Stafford Cripps, one of the great and good, for that enjoyable period of austerity we unnecessarily underwent for years after the War had ended. Sweeties for the weans (and everybody) were rationed and the working man had to find clothing coupons for his working clothes while you luxuriated in your vast Oxfordshire mansion and estate. Bet you did not need an alarm clock to go to toil. But of course it was good for the rest of us, wasn't it?

No. 77 8/8/48

3. The following letter appeared in the Glasgow Evening News on Wednesday, 4th August, 1948:-

"Your correspondents appear to be ignorant of the fact that Glasgow Transport Department is one of the largest rate-payers in the city.

The amount paid in rates last year was £119,335 whilst a further sum of £132,000 was paid to the National Exchequer for income tax, fuel oil tax and vehicle licences. The Department also maintains the highways between the tramway tracks on 135 miles of streets, thus further assisting the rate-payers.

I have visited every large British city recently and have not yet seen a transport service which can compare with Glasgow for service, civility, or cheapness.
Glasgow, W.1."

And this is when our so-wise city fathers were determined to be rid of our much-loved trams.

This was the month also when my favourite tram service to Uddingston ended so that the track could be extended from Knightswood to Blairdardie. The very fine Evening News, like the trams, is long gone. I visited more than a few English cities in 1948 and very much agree with all the nice things the correspondent said about Glasgow being tops. No offence intended, Sassenachs! Nowadays of course bus operators buy castles from the profit that used to benefit the ratepayer.

No. 79 5/9/48

8. The following letter has been received by the General Manager:-

"I have just come back from Glasgow, after a fortnight's visit in charge of a school journey party from North Paddington Secondary School, London, W.9. during which we had occasion to travel very frequently on your trams, and I now pay a sincere tribute to the transport men of Glasgow whom we met on our travels.

We were a party of fifty-two, all told, staying in Maryhill, and there was no day during our stay on which some or all of our party did not make at least two journeys on a tram. On many occasions we had to invade them at most inconvenient times; yet it is literally true to say that we never on any single occasion met with anything but courtesy, cheerfulness, and positive kindness from the conductors who had to cope with us. I personally have used trams and buses in all the principal cities and towns of Britain, and I have never experienced such helpfulness from transport officials as in Glasgow.

I see that I have mentioned only men. I should, of course, have said "the men and women on Glasgow trams." If our grateful appreciation of their patience and efficiency could be conveyed to them – and especially those on Routes 11, 13, 18, 23 and 40 – we should be very much obliged. They contributed much to the success and pleasure of our visit."

Wonder if that bear was with them? I had, on many, many occasions, the task of taking parties of pupils around the city and we were always, without exception, treated with courtesy and interest. Occasionally entertainment was provided e.g. allowing the children to issue their tickets – a practice greeted with shock, horror, and indignation by some modern tramway preservationists. But things were very much more pleasant in those supposedly unenlightened days.

No. 116 23/4/59

7. When two trams meet at a junction at the same time, the tram going the shorter distance shall proceed first. Where the intersection is on a curve, priority shall be given to the vehicle on the straight track. The practice of some tram drivers wasting time in deciding who should proceed first will not be tolerated.

Prim passengers were sometimes shocked as they imagined that motormen were making rude signs to each other at junctions, when in fact the latter were merely trying to signal the minutes of the arrival time at the next timing point.

No. 117 7/5/50

2. The practice of some conductors cutting notches in shoulder straps, presumably for holding pencils, must be discontinued.

In addition to being charged with the cost of repairs, employees guilty of such an offence shall be liable to disciplinary action.

Sharp and to the point – or pretty blunt

No. 125 24/9/50

3. A number of motorbuses have been damaged to the extent of having holes bored through the roofs of cabins to the upper saloons.

This wilful and senseless practice cannot be tolerated and warning is hereby given that any employee responsible for disfiguring or damaging departmental property in this or any other way will be immediately dismissed from the service.

Could not resist this one as a veteran of the Standard tramcar platform. Extra ventilation was definitely not required on that.

No. 140 18/11/51

6. The undernoted has been abusing the facility of credit fare and conductors are notified that no further facility should be afforded this person:-

Mr. Angelus; various addresses.

Clearly one of the bad angels. But was he a Latin student from the Yoonie?

No.36 12/1/47

14. For some time past consideration has been given to the engagement of a Chiropodist, as it is felt that such a service would be invaluable to the staff, most of whom are on their feet throughout the whole day, and the following arrangements have now been made:

A chiropodist will be in attendance at Govan Depot in the forenoons only on Mondays, Wednesdays, and Fridays, commencing Monday, 13th January, 1947. Any employee wishing to avail himself of the facilities offered should apply to the Personnel Department so that a suitable appointment can be made. The charge for this service will be 1s. (5p) per treatment, and must be paid at the time of making the appointment. It is hoped that the efforts made by the Management in this connection will be appreciated by the staff. The scope of the scheme will depend entirely on the advantage taken of the initial arrangements.

In my own experience the old Glasgow Corporation was caring to its employees as the above bears out. But was the scheme a success, and how long did it last?

No. 47 15/6/47

9. As complaints have been received from intending passengers who have been refused admission to Departmental vehicles, the following extract from Corporation Byelaws is issued for the guidance of employees:-

"No person shall travel in or on any car with loaded firearms or with any article, instrument or implement which may be dangerous or offensive to the passengers"

No mean city indeed – but how was the conductor to know if a firearm was loaded?

No. 48 29/6/47

4. It has been reported that employees are consistently failing to close the lids of time recorder clocks, thereby inviting damage by children and irresponsible persons. The lids of recorder clocks must be securely fastened after use, and employees should note that this instruction must be strictly adhered to.

The instruction was deliberately not adhered to at all and eventually the much disliked "Bundies" were removed.

No. 50 27/7/47

9. The Department has been notified that German prisoners of war in this country who are not classified as ardent Nazis are now permitted to use public transport within five miles of their camp.

How was the poor conductor to know whether the POW was or wasn't an ardent Nazi or was or wasn't within bounds?

No. 78 23/8/48

No. 8. The wearing of head scarves is contrary to Department instructions, and must be discontinued immediately. Disciplinary action will be taken against any employee disregarding this instruction.

I never saw a motorman wearing one – but you never know.

No. 94 27/3/49

2. Drivers are hereby notified that they must not use the cross-over in Castle Street near Kennedy Street, as the trolley wire for this crossover has been removed.

Quite. Non-wired crossovers were used by Edinburgh trams – e.g as at Murrayfield –but then they had the advantage of using trolley poles. Wonder if any one did try to crossover at Castle Street? Knowing GCT motormen it would not surprise me.

No. 102 27/4/49

8. It has been reported that the amount of fuse wire used is out of all proportion to the defects, and that it is being used by the operating staff for purposes for which it is not intended, e.g. to clip cash bags and T.I.M. straps together.

Spare fuses are part of the equipment of a tram for use in an emergency and must not be used for any other purpose.

They must have blown an awful lot of fuses in 46 Bath Street.

No. 112 5/2/50

12. The General Manager is pleased to note that a letter has been received from Mr. J. McAlercy on behalf of the Explorers' Club, Glasgow, commending all concerned in the various outings arranged for the children during last year.

Wonder if they explored the back-courts of Lyons Street – where conditions then were such that it was hard to believe they existed in a supposedly civilised society.

No. 132 18/2/51

6. The attention of drivers of tramcars and trolleybuses is directed to the Minister of Transport Regulations as to speed, full details of which are contained in the Rule Book, pages 100-109. Drivers are hereby instructed to make themselves acquainted with every detail contained in these pages relative to the speed at which vehicles will be driven, and it should further be noted that the maximum speed on any point of the system is 25 m.p.h., and the maximum speed on sections not detailed in the rule book is 20 m.p.h.

To obviate a recurrence of a case heard in the Sheriff Court recently, when a tram driver was fined for driving his tram at a speed of over 25 m.p.h., drivers are hereby warned that the speeds contained in the rule book must be adhered to and the regulations as laid down by the Minister of Transport adhered to.

All very fine! But I never saw a speedometer on a Glasgow tram. How were the motormen to know their exact speed? Wonder why the Union lawyer in the case referred to did not put forward that defence? The balancing speed of a Glasgow Standard was reckoned to be 28 m.p.h. but on the last demonic journey depot-wards the speed touched seemed much higher than that. I always wondered at the dear old four-wheelers staying on the track.

No. 10. It has been reported that some tramcars are being driven at excessive speed on the private track between Langloan and Baillieston.

Tram drivers are warned that police action may follow any further offence of this nature.

Coming home on RAF leave I often caught Coatbridge Depot's last "Standard" of the night which connected with a waiting Parkhead car at Baillieston. Alton Towers never had a thrill like that. Incidentally there was no re-booking at Baillieston for the change of tram. Have never seen that unusual practice mentioned anywhere.

No. 139 3/6/51

7. Conductors are instructed that T.I.M. Ticket Rolls must be used to the end to prevent unnecessary waste.

Conductors are also instructed that they must on no account give rolls of paper to children, as complaints have been made that children are causing a nuisance with them, particularly in the vicinity of depots.

No excuse of course for encouraging litter – but there could be a real problem in the use of ticket issuing machine paper rolls. Often sod's law would decree that the end of roll warning marks would start to appear just before coming to stops where experience taught that a very large load of passengers could be expected. It just was not practical to wait until the middle of the bedlam to start a ticket roll change – hence there often was good reason in the conductor's opinion for not using the paper roll until the due end.

No. 143 19/8/51

5. Due to the steady increase in the cost of food throughout the current year it has been necessary to increase the cost of tea to 2d per cup and coffee to 3d per cup.

All other prices, as shown on Canteen Price List dated 30th May, 1951 remain unchanged.

5 New Pence equalled 12 old pennies so even the increased prices were most reasonable.

No. 149 16/12/51

7. It has been noted that conductors are not carrying out the instructions regarding the renewing of ribbons in Ultimate machines.

The ribbon after being used for the first day should be advanced 1/4 inch; at the end of the second day the ribbon should be advanced a further 1/4 inch; and at the end of the third day it should be taken out and replaced so that the other side can be used in the same way for the next three days.

After six days a new ribbon which is obtainable from the depot or garage office must be fitted.

Bet you didn't know that?

No.150 30/12/51

7. Conductors are reminded that Red Tokens marked "Two Stage Token" are only valued 1½d. and do NOT entitle the holder to travel two stages.

And you thought it was easy conducting a tramcar.

No. 151 13/1/52

4. In future conductresses, who are getting married and wish to be retained in the service of the Department after marriage, must make written application to be retained at least 14 days before the date of marriage, to the Personnel Department.

To enable department records to be kept up-to-date, women, who are so retained, must call at the Personnel Department within 14 days of marriage with their marriage certificate.

Short honeymoons in the Fifties!

No. 157 11/5/52

6. The attention of all staff is drawn to the following recent court cases:-

On 30th April, 1952, a conductor was sentenced to 30 days imprisonment without the option, when he pleaded guilty to a charge of Fraud against the Department. He had no previous conviction.

On 2nd May, 1952, a conductress was fined £10 or 60 days imprisonment, when she pleaded guilty to a charge of embezzling £7 15s 5 1/2d from the Department by fraudulent manipulation of her tickets.

As a frequent passenger I occasionally saw fraud happening. There were various methods used. Send an envelope for full descriptions.

No. 161 7/9/52

12. The attention of all conductors is drawn to the rule which states "No person shall bring into or upon, or convey or cause or permit to be conveyed, in or on any vehicle, any bundle of clothing, or any article or thing, tending to communicate any infectious or contagious disease, or any dead body, or any article of an offensive or dangerous character, or of a bulk or description which may interfere with the comfort of any passenger; and such article or thing, if introduced, may, along with the person introducing the same, who shall forfeit his fare, be removed summarily from such vehicle by the conductor."

Conductors will please note that this bye-law must be strictly adhered to.

Wonder what "thing" the lawyer who obviously composed the above paeon had in mind? How was the conductor to know if the "thing" was infectious or contagious? I knew that some Glasgow businesses were sustained by making free use of the Standard's front platform to transfer goods, but I never came across an undertaker trying to make use of that service! I did once see an angry motorman volubly ejecting a pedlar with voluminous bags from a Rome MRS tram – but never witnessed a Glasgow eviction.

No. 168 8/2/53

9. There are a number of vacancies for pipers and drummers in the Transport Pipe Band. Employees interested in joining should make application in writing to the Personnel Superintendent, 46 Bath Street.

It should be noted that pipers are required to supply their own bagpipes.

Was it a green, white and orange tartan. Doubt it!!!

No. 171 29/3/53

3. Coronation tramcars are now in operation on Service 7.

Drivers are hereby warned that should a Coronation Mark II tramcar be waiting in Govan Road to enter Golspie Street when a train from Fairfield's Shipyard to the Mineral Yard is approaching on the city track, the driver of the Coronation tramcar must not proceed until the train has passed.

Did the Department ever refer to Coronation Mark II cars as "Cunarders"?

No. 181 13/12/53

10. Permission has been granted to Students to make collections on Departmental vehicles on Saturday, 30th January 1954.

Notice is hereby given that students must leave the vehicles immediately the collection has been completed. Any student failing to do so, or occupying a seat, must pay the ordinary fare.

Students are not allowed to travel on the platform of a vehicle, especially the driver's platform.

Miserable old department. But happily most green staff enjoyed having the students on board – (as did most passengers?), and interpreted the instructions with great generosity. One not-so-bright specimen from Gilmorehill had a great time with his ice-axe setting the Woodlands Road points for the oncoming motormen till cautioned by a blue-coated minion of the law. Blush! Blush! Remember those corny "rag day" characters Philip McCann, Poppa Bobbin, and Mustapha Tanner? And in Glasgow King Farouk and Groucho Marx were much in evidence.

Happy, happy days.

No. 187 16/5/54

5. It has been agreed to deduct a contribution of 2d. per week (remember 12d. = 5p.) for Manor House hospital and 1d. per week for Red Cross, from the wages of all employees in the Traffic Section, excepting those who notify the Depot or Garage Clerk that they do not wish to contribute.

And it was necessary to opt out of paying Union Dues which could be unpopular. I wasn't anti-union but my father was – so I was in trouble either way.

No. 194 7/11/54

2. A letter has been received from the Director of Education relative to an incident involving a child who had the misfortune to lose her purse while travelling to school.

The conductress of the bus on which she was travelling, without hesitation, removed her from the vehicle, despite the fact that it was raining heavily and she was a long way from home.

Such callous treatment cannot be permitted and employees are hereby notified that, in all cases where a school child is unable to produce the fare, a credit slip must be issued allowing the child to complete the journey.

Conductors failing to obey this instruction will render themselves to severe disciplinary action.

Sounds awful doesn't it. But I wonder. Passengers on the vehicle surely would have interfered in such a situation. As I often found to my cost, young people could hang you out to dry for their own twisted reasons. Cynical me wonders what that girl was really up to. It is also strange-sounding to our ears that a conductress is alleged to have committed the offence – but conductors are warned!!

No. 200 6/2/55

9. A communication has been received from British European Airways pointing out that conductors on tramcars between Renfrew and Paisley are directing passengers to leave the vehicles at Newmains Road, for the airport at Renfrew.

Conductors should note that any passengers going to the Airport on this particular route should leave at the Broadloan or Porterfield Rd. stop, as this is the nearest approach to the Airport.

Off to the continent via GCT! Glasgow's trams once also served Abbotsinch. Did any other UK tram system serve two different airports? But "on this particular route" is puzzling. What was the other route?

No. 212 24/6/55

9. Considerable damage is being caused to hand rails and roof panels on vehicles by persons swinging on the hand rails and treating the vehicle as a gymnasium.

This practice must cease and the co-operation of all employees is requested in preventing damage of this nature.

Have to confess that I could easily traverse the top deck of a "Standard" and down to the back platform without my feet touching the floor. (Sometimes I wasn't trying to do it!) It was much harder to accomplish that feat on a Coronation. But as to roof damage – it wasn't me. I was only about nine and a half stones then – what with "The Yellow Peril" et al. And you thought that aerobics was a modern notion!

No. 215 14/10/56

13. A letter has been received from a passenger who has been crippled with arthritis for some years and who normally travels by tram service 29 or motorbus service 1A between St. Vincent Street and Gartocher Rd.

This gentleman would like to express his thanks for the kindness and consideration shown to him by staff and officials operating these services.

The General Manager would also like to record his appreciation of the treatment this gentleman has received from the staff.

So the great man did not know that tram service 29 (the Department could never make up its mind whether to write "route" or "service") did not operate between St. Vincent Street and Gartocher Road?

No. 219 10/2/57

11. Although the carriage of loaded firearms is prohibited on this Department's vehicles, conductors will please note that uniformed members of H.M. Forces will be permitted to travel with firearms, these being presumed to be unloaded.

Presumed!!

12. With the establishment of a camp at Aberfoyle for Hungarian refugees, it is likely that some of the inmates will find their way to Glasgow, particularly at the week-ends. As their knowledge of English is in most cases very slight, members of the staff are asked to note that a centre has been established at the Lyric Theatre, Sauchiehall St., where interpreters will be available and you are requested, should the occasion arise, to direct refugees to the centre.

But Puskas, Hideguti, Kosciz, Czibor et al never came – to our great disappointment.

No.222 12/5/57

15. The following letter which will be of interest to the staff in Maryhill, has been received from Mr. J. F. Patel, B.Sc. (Vet.), Hons., M.R.C.V.S.:-

"It gives me great pleasure in writing this letter of thanks at the time of my departure from this country. I wish to offer my hearty thanks to you for offering a job of conductor in your Department during the past nine months of my vacation period. I was working in Maryhill Depot for all of this time and I was very happy there. All the workers, officials and depot clerks there gave me most kind treatment and co-operation. I would like you, sir, to please convey my thanks to the officials of that Depot. On this occasion of my departure I feel sorry to leave the job as I was quite happy and pleased with my work and colleagues. The impressions about efffcient working of G.C.T. Department of Glasgow will always remain in my mind for years to come."

What a lovely letter. Wish I had done something like that to thank Dennistoun Depot – but I am sorry to write that I just took the good treatment I received for granted – as something Glaswegians did to each other.

Mr. Patel would have been an even more useful GCT employee 60 years earlier.

No. 228 19/1/58

4. A letter has been received form a blind lady residing in the south side of Glasgow thanking the staff for the good care that they have always taken of her when travelling.

(Of course in our marvellous days the game is to throw bangers at a blind lady's Guide Dog and so terrify her and a helpful and helpless dumb animal).

6. A letter has ... been received from an ex-employee in the Underground section:-

"Once Rudyard Kipling said – 'East is east and west is west and never the twain shall meet'.

Our management has an answer to this saying, for it has succeeded in welding the eastern and western green staff together as a working unit an unique responsibility in the scheme of human relations. The Depot Clerk has shown a great skill in enlivening the atmosphere and creating a communal harmony among both foreign and local green staff.

As I regret departing I pay my hearty thanks to all for the favours and treatment I had during the short period of my service and I do hope my colleagues will go on showing enthusiasm in their work and keep the wheels turning."

M.Z. SYED (Ex Driver)

And I thought RK was talking about Parkhead and Ibrox – but I wonder what that Underground Depot Clerk got up to?

No. 236 11/1/59

13. The following letter has been received from the Secretary of the 33rd (Camphill) Municipal Ward Committee:-

"At a meeting of our Ward Committee it was decided that I convey to you our appreciation of those members of your uniformed staffs who stuck to their posts during the heavy fog in the city on Monday, 1st December 1958, and continued under great difficulties to drive and conduct their vehicles.

Particular reference was made to the evening services at tea-time when the darkness and fog together made conditions even worse than they had been during daylight. Quite a few of our members said how grateful they were to your drivers and conductors for bringing them safely back from town to their homes in spite of the extreme weather conditions .

I have much pleasure in obeying the wishes of my Ward Committee in this matter."

The General Manager would also like to thank those members of the staff who continued to operate their vehicles in extremely adverse conditions.

I well remember that particular night. I followed trams from Langside to Garrowhill and was mightily relieved when I reached Garrowhill Drive. It was a most difficult task to find the correct tram to follow. In thick fog bus conductors would precede their vehicle with a torch. They were brave fellows. On one occasion we were coming down Carntynehall Road on the old 10a bus – preceded by the conductor who was looking for kerbs. We still, somehow, ended up in Lightburn Road. Thank God for the Clean Air Acts.

GCT-HEE!

Despairing Depot Clerk: "Don't you see that big notice there – "ALL HATS MUST BE WORN?"
Sloppy Stroppy Motorman: "Ma hat is worn. It's in the hoose wie a big hole in it."

Irate Inspector: "You must have your hat on a car!"
Clippie: "It is. Ah left it oan a twinty-three gaun tae Airdrie."

Clippie in the Black-out:" Whit on earth happened tae ra wee lamp-lighter?
Whin Ah sclimbed up ra stairs, he wiz staunen there oan ra platform, quite ra thing, hauden his pole?"

Happy Chappie; "Diz this caur go tae ra Palais, then, hen?"
Nippy Clippie "Naw! Disnae fancy ra shimmy, Jimmy."

Posh intending passenger: "Excuse me, conductor. Is this car proceeding to Enniesland"
Student Conductor "Ectually, old thing, we are only meandering to Kailvinside."
(Who'd better be nameless!).

Passenger, laden with luggage, alighting from a 15 at Central Station:
"Well! Thank God that is the worst part of the journey over!"
Puzzled Conductor; "Why? Whaur ye gaun?"
Much relieved passenger; "Egypt."

Tram at terminus: Conductress is sitting at her end of the car manicuring her nails. Motorman is sitting at his end concentrating on the sporting pages. Four men race up to the waiting tram and jump on. Breathlessly the first says to the conductress, "Whit aboot that, hen? Ah'm twinty years older than any o'them an' ah beat them to the caur!"
Without looking up the conductress replies: "See him up there. He's the wan that gies oot the prizes."

These words of wisdom assisted by W. Guthrie.

FULL LIST OF ROUTES
A-Z & RP

A
SPRINGFIELD ROAD and DALMUIR WEST

SPRINGFIELD ROAD	23
LONDON ROAD	24
PARKHEAD CROSS	25
FLEMING STREET	26
BELLGROVE STREET	27
HIGH STREET	28
BUCHANAN STREET	29
WELLINGTON ST.	30
ST. GEORGE'S CROSS	31
PARK ROAD	32
BYRES ROAD	33
HYNDLAND ROAD	34
WHITTINGEHAME DRIVE	35
ANNIESLAND	36
KNIGHTSWOOD RD.	37
LINCOLN AVENUE	38
BLAWARTHILL RD.	39
FERRY ROAD	40
DOCK STREET	41
BON ACCORD ST.	42
L.M.S. RAILWAY BRIDGE	43
BEARDMORE ST.	44
DALMUIR WEST	45

B
AIRDRIE and FERGUSLIE MILLS

AIRDRIE	7
AIRDRIE CROSS	8
RALSTON STREET	9
COATDYKE (LOCKS STREET)	10
JACKSON STREET	11
WHITELAW FOUNTAIN	12
DUNDYVAN ROAD	13
COATBRIDGE (WOODSIDE ST.)	14
DRUMPELLIER LODGE	15
DRUMPARK FARM	16
BARGEDDIE	17
RHINDS	18
BAILLIESTON (157 ALAIN STREET)	19
BAILLIESTON (NORTH)	20
BARRACHNIE ROAD	21
CULROSS STREET	22
CHESTER STREET	23
MUIRYFAULD DRIVE	24
PARKHEAD CROSS	25
WHITEVALE STREET	26
BELIGROVE STREET	27
GLASGOW CROSS	28
ARGYLE STREET	29
TRADESTON STREET	30
ADMIRAL STREET	31
PERCY STREET	32
BROOMLOAN ROAD	33
JURA STREET	34
HALFWAY	35
FIFE AVENUE	36
CROOKSTON ROAD	37
RALSTON (EAST GATE)	38
OLDHALL	39
HAWKHEAD ROAD	40
M'KERRELL STREET	41
PAISLEY CROSS	42
CASTLE STREET	43
FERGUSLIE MILLS	44

C
CLARKSTON and KIRKLEE

CLARKSTON	20
STAMPERLAND AVE.	21
NETHERLEE	22
CATHCART CEMETERY GATE	23
CATHCART RAILWAY BRIDGE	24
BATTLEFIELD	25
QUEEN'S PARK GATE	26
EGLINTON TOLL	27
COOK STREET -	28
ARGYLE STREET	29
WELLINGTON ST.	30
CHARING CROSS	31
RADNOR STREET	32
LAWRENCE STREET	33
Via HYNDLAND-	
156 HYNDLAND RD	34
KIRKLEE	35
Via BYRES ROAD-	
KIRKLEE	34
OVERLAPPING STATIONS-	
BYRES ROAD	1
HYNDLAND ROAD	2

D
AIRDRIE and KNIGHTSWOOD

AIRDRIE	7
AIRDRIE CROSS	8
RALSTON STREET	9
COATDYKE (LOCKS STREET)	10
JACKSON STREET	11
WHITELAW FOUNTAIN	12
DUNDYVAN ROAD	13
COATBRIDGE (WOODSIDE ST.)	14
DRUMPELLIER LODGE	15
DRUMPARK FARM	16
BARGEDDIE	17
RHINDS	18
BAILLIESTON (157 MAIN STREET)	19
BAILLIESTON (NORTH)	20
BARRACHNIE ROAD	21
CULROSS STREET	22
CHESTER STREET	23
MUIRYFAULD DRIVE	24
BEARDMORE'S OFFICES	25
FLEMING STREET	26
BELLGROVE STREET	27
HIGH STREET	28
BUCHANAN STREET	29
WELLINGTON ST.	30
ST. GEORGE'S CROSS	31
PARK ROAD	32
BYRES ROAD	33
HYNDLAIND ROAD	34
WHITTINGEHAME DRIVE	35
ANNIESLAND	36
KNIGHTSWOOD	37

E
MOSSPARK and UNIVERSITY

MOSSPARK	21
AULDBAR ROAD	22
DUMBRECK FARM	23
ERSKINE AVENUE	24
NITHSDALE CROSS	25
SHIELDS ROAD	26
EGLINTON TOLL	27
COOK STREET	28

ARGYLE STREET 29
WELLINGTON ST. 30
CHARING CROSS 31
UNIVERSITY 32

F
BURNSIDE OR RUTHERGLEN and DALMUIR WEST

BURNSIDE 22
STONELAW DRIVE 23
STONELAW ROAD or RUTHER-
   GLEN 24
STEWART'S & LLOYDS 25
557 DALMARNOCK RD. 26
BRIDGETON CROSS 27
KENT STREET 28
QUEEN STREET 29
ANDERSTON CROSS 30
FINNIESTON ST. 31
CHURCH STREET 32
MERKLAND STREET 33
BALSHAGRAY AVE. - 34
WHITEINCH 35
SCOTSTOUN 36
BLAWARTHILL RD. 37
FERRY ROAD 38
DOCK STREET 39
CLYDEBANK
   (BON-ACCORD ST.) 40
L.M.S. RAILWAY BRIDGE 41
BEARDMORE ST. 42
DALMUIR WEST 43

G
LAMBHILL or SPRINGBURN and LINTHOUSE

LAMBHILL 24
POSSIL SCHOOL 25
SARACEN CROSS 26
SPRINGBURN ROAD 24
SPRUCE STREET 25
SARACEN CROSS 26
RAGLAN STREET 27
MAITLAND STREET 28
ARGYLE STREET 29
TRADESTON STREET 30
ADMIRAL STREET 31
LORNE SCHOOL 32
SUMMERTON ROAD 33
GOVAN CROSS 34
HOLMFAULDHEAD DRIVE 35

H
LANGSIDE and JORDANHILL

LANGSIDE 25
QUEEN'S PARK GATE 26
EGLINTON TOLL 27
COOK STREET 28
ARGYLE STREET 29
WELLINGTON ST. 30
CHARING CROSS 31
RADNOR STREET 32
LAWRENCE STREET 33
156 HYNDLAND RD. 34
BROOMHILL CROSS 35
JORDANHILL 36

J
MILLERSTON or ALEXANDRA PARK and CRAIGTON ROAD

MILLERSTON 20
HOGGANFIELD 21
RIDDRIE 22
GOUGH STREET 23
ALEXANDRA PARK 24
MILLERSTON ST. 25
BELLGROVE STN. 26
BRIDGETON CROSS 27
MINEIL STREET 28
CROWN STREET 29
TRADESTON ST. 30
ADMIRAL STREET 31
LORNE SCHOOL 32
SUMMERTON ROAD 33
GOVAN CROSS 34
CROSSLOAN ROAD OR
   HOLMFAULDHEAD DRIVE 35
CRAIGTON ROAD OR
   SHIELDHALL 36
SHIELS FARM 37
HILLINGTON ROAD 38
RENFREW CROSS 39
PORTERFIELD ROAD 40

K
KEPPOCHHILL ROAD and RENFREW

KEPPOCHHILL RD. 25
PINKSTON ROAD 26
RAGLAN STREET 27
MAITLAND STREET 28
ARGYLE STREET 29
TRADESTON ST. 30

ADMIRAL STREET 31
LORNE SCHOOL OR PERCY
   STREET 32
SUMMERTON RD OR BROOM-
   LOAN RD. 33
GOVAN CROSS 34
HOLMFAULDHEAD DRIVE 35
SHIELDHALL 36
SHIELS FARM 37
HILLINGTON ROAD 38
RENFREW CROSS 39
PORTERFIELD RD. 40

L
AUCHENSHUGGLE and DALMUIR WEST

AUCHENSHUGGLE 23
MAUKINFAULD RD. 24
1277 LONDON ROAD 25
FRASER STREET 26
BRIDGETON CROSS 27
KENT STREET 28
QUEEN STREET 29
ANDERSTON CROSS 30
FINNIESTON ST. 31
CHURCH STREET 32
MERKLAND STREET 33
BALSHAGRAY AVE. 34
WHITEINCH 35
SCOTSTOUN 36
BLAWARTHILL RD. 37
FERRY ROAD 38
DOCK STREET 39
CLYDEBANK
   BON-ACCORD ST. 40
L.M.S. RAILWAY BRIDGE 41
BEARDMORE ST. 42
DALMUIR WEST 43

M
MOUNT FLORIDA and MILNGAVIE

MOUNT FLORIDA 25
DIXON AVENUE 26
AIKENHEAD ROAD 27
CLELAND STREET 28
TRONGATE 29
36 WEST NILE ST. 30
1 NEW CITY ROAD 31
NORTH WOODSIDE ROAD 32
KELVINSIDE AVE. 23
GAIRBRAID AVE. 34
MARYHILL
   (CALDERCUILT RD) 35
ACRE ROAD 36

CANNIESBURN 37
HILLFOOT 38
REID AVENUE 39
MILNGAVIE 41

N
SINCLAIR DRIVE and GAIRBRAID AVENUE or MARYHILL

SINCLAIR DRIVE 24
BATTLEFIELD RD. 25
QUEEN'S PARK GATE 26
EGLINTON TOLL 27
CLELAND STREET 28
TRONGATE 29
36 WEST NILE ST. 30
1 NEW CITY ROAD 31
CEDAR STREET 32
KELVINSIDE AVE. 33
GAIRBRAID AVE. 34
MARYHILL
   (CALDERCUILT RD.) 35

O
RUTHERGLEN or OATLANDS and KIRKLEE

RUTHERGLEN 23
WHITE'S WORKS 24
SHAWFIELD DRIVE 25
BRAEHEAD STREET 26
129 CROWN STREET 27
GLASGOW CROSS 28
QUEEN STREET OR UNION
   STREET 29
DOUGLAS STREET 30
CHARING CROSS 31
PARK ROAD 32
BYRES ROAD 33
KIRKLEE 34

P
RENFREW FERRY and MARYHILL or MILNGAVIE

RENFREW FERRY 1
HIGH STREET 2
PORTERFIELD RD. 3
ARKLESTON ROAD 4
GALLOWHILL 5
HAMILTON STREET 6
PAISLEY CROSS 7
ESPEDAIR STREET 8
LOCHFIELD ROAD 9
SOUTHFIELD AVE 10

STONEYBRAE 11
CROSS-STOBS 12
BARRHEAD (ROBERTSON ST.) 13
317 MAIN STREET 14
TOWER RAIS 15
PARKHOUSE 16
DARNLEY HOSPITAL 17
RANGES 18
SPEIRSBRIDGE 19
THORNLIEBANK PRINT
   WORKS 20
THORNLIEBANK RAILWAY
   STATION 21
BEMERSYDE AVE. 22
POLLOCKSHAWS WEST 23
GREENVIEW ST. 24
SHAWLANDS CROSS 25
REGENT PARK SQ. 26
EGLINTON TOLL 27
CLELAND STREET - 28
TRONGATE 29
36 WEST NILE ST. 30
1 NEW CITY ROAD 31
NORTH WOODSIDE ROAD 32
KELVINSIDE AVE. 33
GAIRBRAID AVE. 34
MARYHALL
   (CALDERCULT RD.) 35
ACRE ROAD 36
CANNIESBURN 37
HILLFOOT 38
REID AVENUE 39
BURNBRAE 40
MILNGAVIE 41

Q
MOUNT FLORIDA and PAISLEY RD. TOLL

MOUNT FLORIDA 25
DIXON AVENUE 26
POLLOKSHAWS RD. 27
ALBERT DRIVE 28
PAISLEY RD. TOLL 29

R
ROUKEN GLEN and BISHOPBRIGGS or MILLERSTON

Via POLLOKSHAWS-
ROUKEN GLEN 19
THORNLIEBANK PRINT WORKS
  20
THORNLIEBANK STATION 21
BEMERSYDE AVE. 22
POLLOKSHAWS WEST 23

GREENVIEW STREET 24
SHAWLANDS CROSS 25
   Via KILMARNOCK RD-
ROUKN GLEN 19
EASTWOOD TOLL 20
GIFFNOCK RAILWAY STATION 21
GIFFNOCK FARM 22
MERRYLEE ROAD 23
CORROUR ROAD 24
SHAWLANDS CROSS 25
REGENT PARK SQ. 26
EGLINTON TOLL 27
COOK STREET 28
ARGYLE STREET 29
HANOVER STREET 30
   Via SPRINGBURN-
181 CASTLE ST. 31
PETERSHILL ROAD 32
BALGRAY HILL 33
HUNTERSHILL ST. 34
STUART DRIVE 35
BISHOPBRIGGS 36
   Via ALEXANDRA PARK-
4 MONKLAND ST. 31
CRAIGPARK STREET 32
ALEXANDRA PARK 33
GOUGH STREET 34
RIDDRIE 35
HOGGANFIELD 36
MILLERSTON 37

S
NETHERLEE or MOUNT FLORIDA and SPRINGBURN

NETHERLEE 22
CATHCART CEMETERY GATE 23
CATHCART RAILWAY BRIDGE 24
MOUNT FLORIDA 25
DIXON AVENUE 26
AIKENHEAD ROAD 27
RUTHERGLEN RD. 28
GLASGOW CROSS 29
DUKE STREET or
   CATHEDRAL ST. 30
181 CASTLE ST. 31
PETERSHILL ROAD 32
BALGRAY HILL 33

U
UDDINGSTON and FERGUSLIE MILLS

UDDINGSTON 15
STATION ROAD 16
BOGG KNOWE 17

CLYDESIDE COLLIERY	18	SCOTSTOUN	36		
BROOMHOUSE	19	BLAWARTHILL RD.	37		
MOUNT VERNON RAILWAY STATION	20	FERRY ROAD	38		
ARDOCH VILLA	21	DOCK STREET	39		
41 HAMILTON RD.	22	CLYDEBANK (BON-ACCORD ST.)	40		
CAUSEWAYSIDE ST.	23	L.M.S. RAILWAY BRIDGE	41		
MAUKINFAULD RD.	24	BEARDMORE ST.	42		
PARKHEAD CROSS	25	DALMUIR WEST	43		

Z
RIDDRIE or ALEXANDRA PARK and SCOTSTOUN or DAL1lUIR WEST

WHITEVALE STREET	26			MILLERSTON	21
BELLGROVE STREET	27			HOGGANFIELD-	22
GLASGOW CROSS	28			RIDDRIE	23
ARGYLE STREET	29			GOUGH STREET	24
TRADESTON STREET	30			ALEXANDRA PARK	25
ADMIRAL STREET	31			CRAIGPARK STREET	26
PERCY STREET	32			4 MONKLAND ST.	27
BROOMLOAN ROAD	33			HANOVER STREET	28
JURA STREET	34			WELLINGTON ST.	29

X
CAMBUSLANG and ANNIESLAND

HALFWAY	35	CAMBUSLANG	21	CHARING CROSS	30
FIFE AVENUE	36	BUCHANAN DRIVE	22	RADNOR STREET	31
CROOKSTON ROAD	37	EASTFIELD SCHOOL	23	CHURCH STREET	32
RALSTON (EAST GATE)	38	CLYDEVIEW PLACE	24	MERKLAND STREET	33
OLDHALL	39	STEWARTS' & LLOYDS'	25	BALSHAGRAY AVE.	34
HAWKHEAD ROAD	40	557 DALMARNOCK RD.	26	WHITEINCH	35
M'KERRELL STREET	41	BRIDGETON CROSS	27	SCOTSTOUN	36
PAISLEY CROSS	42	KENT STREET	28	BLAWARTHILL RD.	37
CASTLE STREET	43	QUEEN STREET	29	FERRY ROAD	38
FERGUSLIE MILLS	44	DOUGLAS STREET	30	DOCK STREET	39
		FINNIESTON ST.	31	CLYDEBANK (BON-ACCORD ST.)	40
		CHURCH STREET	32	L.M.S. RAILWAY BRIDGE	41

V
POLMADIE and PROVANMILL

		MERKLAND STREET	33	BEARDMORE ST.	42
		BROOMHILL CROSS	34	DALMUIR WEST	43
		SOUTHBRAE LANE	35		
POLMADIE	26	ANNIESLAND	36		
AIKENHEAD ROAD	27				
RUTHERGLEN RD.	28				

R. P.
CLYDEBANK and DUNTOCHER

GLASGOW CROSS	29				

Y
BURNSIDE and SPRINGBURN

DUKE STREET OR CATHEDRAL ST.	30			GLASGOW ROAD	40
181 CASTLE STREET	31	BURNSIDE	22	SECOND AVENUE	41
BLOCHAIRN ROAD	32	STONELAW DRIVE	23	WILLIAMSON ST.	42
617 GARNGAD ROAD	33	RUTHERGLEN	24	CLEDDENS ROAD	43
PROVANMILL	34	WHITE'S WORKS	25	DUNTOCHER	44
		FRENCH STREET	26		

W
KEPPOCHHILL ROAD and WHITEINCH

		BRIDGETON CROSS	27		
		KENT STREET	28		
		QUEEN STREET	29		
KEPPOCHHILL ROAD	27	DOUGLAS STREET	30		
PINKSTON ROAD	28	CHARING CROSS	31		
GARSCUBE ROAD	29	NORTH WOODSIDE ROAD	32		
CHARING CROSS	30	KELVINSIDE AVE.	33		
FINNIESTON ST.	31	COLGRAIN STREET OR GAIR-BRAID AVE.	34		
CHURCH STREET	32	BALMORE ROAD OR CALDER-CUILT RD.	35		
MERKLAND STREET	33	SPRUCE STREET	36		
BALSHAGRAY AVE.	34	SPRINGBURN ROAD	37		
WHITEINCH	35				

Coronation in Shettleston Road/Rigby Street on the last day of 23 service. This is where 1145 had its accident and consequent fatal fire after being involved in a collision with a Beardmore's lorry.

CLOSING OF SHETTLESTON ROAD
AT RAILWAY BRIDGE, SANDYHILLS

From Monday, 18th Jany., until further notice, the ROAD WILL BE CLOSED to all Vehicular Traffic.

PASSENGERS who have booked through will CHANGE TRAMS and complete their journey on production of the ticket issued.

46 Bath Street, January, 1937

CORPORATION TRANSPORT

JAMES N. WILSON, General Manager

Notice of closure of Sandyhills railway bridge. *(see page 28)*

SOME OF THE NAMES THAT APPEARED ON GLASGOW TRAM-CAR DESTINATION SCREENS

Each depot had its own particular set of screens.
The fonts used to print the screens varied from time to time.
Destinations used in service by the author are marked *

ABBOTSINCH
AIRDRIE*
AIRDRIE CROSS*
ALEXANDRA PARK*
ANDERSTON CROSS
ANNIESLAND*
ARDEN
ARDOCH GROVE
AUCHENSHUGGLE

BAILLIESTON*
BALMORE RD.
BARGEDDIE*
BARRACHNIE
BARRACKS GATE
BARRHEAD
BARRHEAD CENTRE
BARSHAW
BATTLEFIELD
BATTLE PLACE
BELLAHOUSTON*
BILSLAND DRIVE
BISHOPBRIGGS*
BLAIRDARDIE*
BON ACCORD ST.
BOTANIC GARDENS*
BOTHWELL ST.
BRAIDS ROAD
BRIDGETON CROSS*
BRIDGE STREET*
BROOMHILL CROSS
BROOMHOUSE

BROOMLOAN RD.
BURNSIDE

CAMBUSLANG*
CANNIESBURN
CARMYLE
CARNTYNE*
CARNWADRIC*
CASTLE STREET*
CATHCART
CAUSEYSIDE
CELTIC PARK
CHARING CROSS*
CHURCH ST.
CITY CENTRE*
CLARKSTON
CLYDEBANK*
COATBRIDGE*
COATBRIDGE DEPOT*
COATDYKE*
COLSTON DRIVE
COMMERCE ST.
CORKERHILL ROAD
COUNTY SQUARE
CRAIGTON ROAD
CROOKSTON
CROSSHILL
CROSSTOBS
CROWN ST.

DALMUIR*
DALMUIR WEST*

DARNLEY
DENNISTOUN*
DENNISTOUN DEPOT*
DEPOT ONLY
DOUGLAS STREET
DUMBRECK

EGLINTON TOLL*
ELDERSLIE
ELDERSLIE DEPOT
ESPEDAIR STREET
EXHIBITION

FALSIDE
FARME CROSS
FERGUSLIE MILLS
FINNIESTON*
FOOTBALL MATCH

GAIRBRAID AVENUE*
GARNGAD
GARROWHILL*
GARRY ST.
GEORGE SQUARE
GIFFNOCK*
GLASGOW CROSS
GLENFIELD
GORBALS
GORBALS CROSS
GOVANHILL
GOVAN CROSS*
GOVAN DEPOT

HALFWAY
HAWKHEAD ROAD
HILLFOOT
HILLINGTON ROAD
HOLMLEA ROAD
HOPE STREET
HYNDLAND

HOLMLEA ROAD
HOPE STREET
HYNDLAND

IBROX
JACKSON STREET*
JAMAICA STREET*
JAMES STREET
JOHNSTONE
JORDANHILL
JURA STREET

KELVINGROVE*
KELVINSIDE*
KELVINSIDE AVENUE*
KELVINSIDE CROSS
KEPPOCHILL ROAD
KILBARCHAN
KILBOWIE ROAD
KILLERMONT
KINNING PARK DEPOT
KIRKLEE
KNIGHTSWOOD*

LAMBHILL
LANGLOAN*
LANGSIDE
LINTHOUSE*
LOCHFIELD ROAD
LONDON ROAD
LORNE SCHOOL*

MARYHILL
MARYHILL DEPOT*
MERRYLEE*
MILLERSTON*

MILNGAVIE
MITCHELL STREET
MOIR STREET*
MONKLAND STREET*
MOSSBANK
MOSSPARK
MOUNT FLORIDA
MOUNT VERNON
NEW CITY ROAD
NEWLANDS*
NORMAL SCHOOL*
NORTH ALBION STREET*
NORTH HANOVER
  STREET*

OATLANDS
OSWALD STREET

PAISLEY CROSS
PAISLEY NORTH
PAISLEY ROAD TOLL
PAISLEY WEST
PARK ROAD
PARKHEAD*
PARKHEAD DEPOT
PARTICK*
PARTICK DEPOT*
POLLOKSHAWS DEPOT
POLLOKSHAWS EAST
POLLOKSHAWS WEST*
POLLOKSHIELDS
POLMADIE
POSSILPARK DEPOT*
POTTERHILL
PRINCES SQUARE
PROVANMILL

QUEEN'S CROSS
QUEEN'S PARK
QUEEN STREET

RENFREW
RENFREW AERODROME
RENFREW CROSS

RENFREW DEPOT
RENFREW FERRY
RENFREW SOUTH
RESERVED
RIDDRIE*
ROBERTS STREET
RUCHILL
RUTHERGLEN
RUTHERGLEN BRIDGE
SANDYFORD
ST. GEORGE'S CROSS*
ST. VINCENT PLACE*
ST. VINCENT STREET*
SARACEN CROSS
SCOTSTOUN*
SCOTSTOUN WEST*
SHAWFIELD
SHAWLANDS*
SHIELDHALL*
SHIELDS RD.
SHETTLESTON*
SINCLAIR DRIVE
SPIERSBRIDGE
SPRINGBANK ROAD
SPRINGBURN*
STOBCROSS FERRRY
STONELAW DRIVE

THORNLIEBANK*
TOLLCROSS
TRONGATE*

UDDINGSTON*

VERNON ST

WHITEINCH*
WHITEVALE
WHITEVALE DEPOT
YOKER*

ZOO

ADAM GORDON

Publisher and dealer in transport literature & ephemera

If you have enjoyed reading this book you may be interested in some of the following titles, many of them being reprints; * = hardback; obtainable from bookshops or direct from the publisher (address below); add 10% for postage and packing up to £4.90 maximum. No post and packing charge for orders of £50 or over.

Tramways of Reading.* H. Jordan, 2nd edition, 96pp, £12

Kidderminster and Stourport Electric Tramway Co Rules and Regulations, 1899, 58pp, £7

My Life in Many States and in Foreign Lands, G.F. Train, autobiography of street railway pioneer, who claimed that Jules Verne based "Around the world in 80 days" upon Train's own voyage; over 350pp, £12

Tramways and Electric Railways in the Nineteenth Century* (Electric Railway Number of Cassier's Magazine, 1899), cloth, over 250pp, £23

Tramways – their construction and working*, D.K. Clark, 2nd edn of 1894, over 750pp, 12 plates and over 400 line drawings, cloth, £32

Edinburgh Corporation Transport Department, timetable of electric tramways and motor buses June 1930, c.2 ¾" by 4 ¾", 72pp, **was £6, but now reduced to £3 due to staples rusting.**

London County Council Tramways Guide to Reopening of Kingsway Subway, 1931, coloured cover and map, 32pp £6

The Cable system of Tramway Traction 1896 – contemporary look at cable systems at home and abroad, 56pp, 6 photo pics and 2 line drawings, £10

The Feltham Car of the Metropolitan Electric and London United Tramways 1931, 18pp £5

The Overhaul of Tramcars, London Transport, 26pp, 1935, £6

Tramway Review*, volumes 1 and 2, issues 1-16, 1950-1954, cloth h/b, includes articles on tramways in East Ham, Nottingham, Luton, Huddersfield, Barking, Sheffield, Oldham, Chester, Ilford, Wallasey, Leyton, Darlington, Cork, Lytham, Walthamstow, Isle of Man and Ireland, £23

Clippie, Z.Katin, a few months in the life of a tram and bus conductress in the war in Sheffield, 124pp £7

London Transport Bus Routes, Central Area No 2 1943, folds out into c.11" by 17" – limited edition of 250 £5

Edinburgh Street Tramways Company Rules and Regulations for the servants, 1883, 56pp, limited edition of 250 £8

London County Council Tramways Motorman's Handbook, as from 1928, 32pp limited edition of 250 £6

The Training of Drivers and Conductors of Buses, Trams and Trolleybuses, London Transport, 1936, 20pp (250) £6

Double Century* by Stan Basnett and Keith Pearson. It comprises updated histories of the Upper Douglas Cable Tramway, and the Douglas Head Marine Drive Tramway. It also includes an appendix on the Cliff Lifts. Ch.4 consists of 'guided walks' along the routes today by Stan Basnett. It has 144 pages, including 8 in colour, and numerous illustrations; red buckram with gold lettering. £15.

My Fifty Years in Transport – A.G. Grundy, 54pp, 26 illus, covers tramways of North Staffordshire, Blackburn, Potteries, Wrexham, and Stalybridge, Hyde, Mossley and Dukinfield. £10

Modern Tramway*, volumes 1 and 2, 1938 and 1939, reprinted and bound together in green cloth, sewn, gold lettering with original Light Rail Transit League logo on front, £38

How to go Tram and Tramway Modelling – David Voice. Second edition of the title first published 16 years ago, now completely rewritten; coloured covers, 168 pages, 150 black & white photographs, 34 diagrams, and an illustrated glossary. £15.

Source Book of Literature Relating to Scottish Tramways – D. Croft & A. Gordon. Includes historical introduction and chronology, books, periodicals and major articles on specific tramway systems, legislation and accident reports, tramway museums and preservation, & rapid transit proposals. 48pp, £5.

Edinburgh's Transport, Volume 2 – The Corporation Years, 1919-1975, by D.L.G.Hunter, 192pp; over 150 illustrations, £20.

The Millennium Guide to Trams in the British Isles, by David Voice. Softback, A5 size, 144 pages, coloured covers, and 45 black & white illustrations, £10

The Douglas Horse Tramway, by Keith Pearson. Softback, A4 size, 96 pages, coloured covers, and over 135 illustrations. £14.50

The Twilight Years of the Glasgow Tram contains over 250 **coloured** views, taken by Douglas McMillan and captioned by Alasdair Turnbull, most of them featuring Glasgow street scenes of the 1950's and early 1960's. A4 ; 144 pages; £25 from bookshops, or £28 inclusive of post and packing direct from the publisher.

All the above published by Adam Gordon, Priory Cottage, Chetwode, Nr. Buckingham, Bucks, MK18 4LB Tel: 01280 848650. [Trade terms, above prices less 35%, or more for multiple copies.]

Do you have anything of transport interest to sell? e.g. books, magazines, photographs, postcards, tickets, timetables, and ephemera – also hardware like ticket machines, racks and punches, enamelled signs, etc. Just ring or write to Adam Gordon above!